For Cynthia and Mags

Welsh

National

Heroes

Alun Roberts

y Lolfa

Thanks to

The National Library of Wales and Colorsport for the photographs

First impression: 2002
Second impression: 2004
© Copyright Alun Roberts and Y Lolfa Cyf., 2002

Cover design: Ceri Jones

ISBN: 0 86243 610 9

Printed on acid free and partly recycled paper
and published and bound in Wales by:
Y Lolfa Cyf., Talybont, Ceredigion SY24 5AP
e-mail ylolfa@ylolfa.com
internet www.ylolfa.com
phone +44 (0)1970 832 304
fax 832 782
isdn 832 813

Contents

Introduction

In 1916, thanks to no small degree to the munificence of Wales' most prominent business tycoon, Viscount Rhondda, David Lloyd George unveiled in Cardiff City Hall a gallery of fine marble statues commemorating eleven Welsh national heroes of the past. Three of them do not feature in this little book (though simply by mentioning them here I have, in effect, included them after all). I am really not convinced by the claims on behalf of Buddug (Boedecea), Queen of the Iceni, who has always been more closely associated in my mind with East Anglia than Wales. Some may argue a perfectly respectable case in favour of the inclusion of Henry Tudor but, despite his authentic Welsh roots and outlook, King Henry VII of England feels somewhat out of place in a book about Welsh national heroes. Nor is there a place for that gallant soldier, Sir Thomas Picton, despite the fact that he is the only Welshman to be buried in St Paul's cathedral.

The other eight however appear in the following pages, Dewi Sant, Hywel Dda, Gerald of Wales, Llywelyn the Last, Dafydd ap Gwilym, Owain Glyndŵr, Bishop William Morgan and William Williams, Pantycelyn; few readers are likely to quarrel with their inclusion. There will, no doubt, be many who will dispute the claims of some of the others featured in the book and will feel, no doubt with some justice, that I have omitted, for no good reason, some obvious Welsh national heroes. For example, some people would have included George Maitland Lloyd Davies, for a short time the Christian Pacifist MP for the University of Wales, or Dr William Price of Llantrisant, Wales' greatest eccentric, father of Iesu Grist and the man who was responsible for the legalisation of cremation. Others would have certainly found a place for Gareth Edwards, Wales' finest modern rugby player. But then, it would have been easy to fill this book with Welsh rugby legends past and present; fortunately they have another book in the *It's Wales* series all to themselves. At the end of the day this book represents my own personal selection, no doubt influenced to some extent by my own interests and prejudices but always by my respect for Wales and its traditions.

It should be emphasised that this particular book is about Welsh heroes, not notables, who are not necessarily the same people. Augustus John, though a very well known Welshman, was probably not really a Welsh national hero in the normal sense of the term, though he certainly painted the portraits of those who were, Lloyd George and Dylan Thomas. The above-mentioned Lord Rhondda, though undoubtedly an eminent Welshman, also just fails to find a place in this book despite surviving the sinking of the Lusitania in 1915, reportedly attracting the newspaper headline "Great National Disaster. D A Thomas saved". There is no place in this book for another Welsh industrial giant, Sir William Thomas Lewis, Baron Merthyr of Senghennydd, once referred to by Sidney and Beatrice Webb as "the best hated man in the Principality". While Lewis would undoubtedly have been much offended by this observation the writer Caradoc Evans, scourge of Welsh Nonconformity, who also fails to make an appearance, positively revelled in his reputation as "the most hated man in Wales".

A lot of reading has gone into the preparation of this volume but space does not permit the inclusion of a comprehensive bibliography. Most of the heroes featured in the following pages are referred to in the splendid *Dictionary of Welsh Biography down to 1940,* produced in Welsh and English, or the supplements, also in Welsh and English, which take the date forward to 1970. The *Oxford Companion to the Literature of Wales,* compiled and edited by Meic Stephens, which also has a Welsh edition, includes many of the same people and provides valuable suggestions for further reading. The best one-volume *History of Wales* is that produced in Welsh and English by John Davies. Gwyn A Williams' *When was Wales?* is another stimulating survey. Four excellent volumes in the History of Wales series produced by the Clarendon Press and the University of Wales Press have so far appeared; R R Davies, *Conquest, Coexistence and Change, Wales 1063-1415*, Glanmor Williams, *Recovery, Reorientation and Reformation, Wales c1415-1642*, Geraint H Jenkins, *The Foundations of Modern Wales 1642-1780* and K O Morgan, *Rebirth of a Nation, Wales 1880-1980*. The monographs in the *Writers of Wales* series, published by the University of Wales Press, are well worth reading, as are the splendidly illustrated volumes in the *Bro a Bywyd* series, written in Welsh about some of the nation's cultural giants of the last century. Jan Morris' evocative *The Matter of Wales: Epic Views of a Small Country* is simply superb.

Alun Roberts

March 2002

DEWI SANT
(6th century)

Not a vast amount is known about Dewi Sant (Saint David), patron saint of Wales. Most of what is known was recorded by the monk Rhygyfarch who wrote *Vita Davidis* around 1094. Though the biography, written centuries after Dewi's death, contained a strong dose of propaganda and fantasy scholars generally agree that it also gave an authentic account of a remarkable man.

When Dewi Sant was born is not known for certain though it is thought to have been around 520 AD. His parents were Sanctus, a king of Ceredigion, and Non and tradition has it that he was born at the site of the present St Non's chapel overlooking St Non's Bay, near St David's. Dewi's early education was at a small Celtic monastery at Henfynyw, south of present day Aberaeron, and was completed at Llanddeusant under Paulinus (whose sight Dewi is said to have restored, one of many miracles attributed to him during his lifetime). Dewi established a monastery in the area where St David's is now, using it as the hub of a network of monasteries he was to establish in west Wales during the sixth century. Monastic life under Dewi was rigorous in the extreme, combining hard labour and earnest contemplation, nourished by little more than bread, herbs and water (he was known as '*Dewi Ddyfrwr*', the water-drinker), though his extreme asceticism and concern for the poor and needy attracted much admiration then and later.

The central event in Dewi's life took place at Llanddewibrefi around 570 AD where, with a white dove sitting on his shoulder, he presided at a synod which played a central role in keeping Celtic Christianity free of

Pelagian heresy. Tradition has it that the earth rose beneath his feet, elevating him above the assembled multitude. Whether it did or not it is clear that Dewi achieved a special prominence at the time, so much so that when he died (possibly in or around 588 AD) there was much anguish among the people. Dewi was buried on the site of the present St David's cathedral (built in 1188) though whether his remains are still preserved in the reliquary behind the main altar must be open to serious doubt.

Dewi's reputation grew during the Middle Ages. *'Sein Daui'* had become a battle cry by the twelfth century and he was canonised under the papacy of Calixtus II (1119–1124). He proclaimed that two pilgrimages to St David's would equal one to Rome, and three would be the equivalent of one pilgrimage to Jerusalem itself. By this time Dewi had achieved the status of Patron Saint of Wales. In 1398 Archbishop Arundel decreed that the Festival of St David should be kept on 1 March, the date on which Dewi was thought to have died. The tradition of St David's Day dinners and the like first arose during the eighteenth century, particularly among the London Welsh societies, and it was Sir Owen M Edwards who inspired the tradition that all schools in Wales should celebrate St David's Day with pageants and plays, and a day's holiday.

HYWEL DDA
(died 950)

Hywel Dda is the only native Welsh ruler on whom History has
bestowed the title 'The Good'. This does not mean that Hywel was an
uniquely saintly character; indeed he was known to be ruthless when the
occasion demanded.

When or where he was born is not known, but he was the grandson
of Rhodri Mawr, the first Welsh ruler to achieve a semblance of
national unity. Hywel first came into prominence in the early years of
the tenth century by gradually extending his family's control over south-
west Wales so that by 920 he was ruler over the whole of Deheubarth.
In 942 he took over control of Gwynedd and Powys as well, thereby
becoming the effective ruler of virtually the whole of Wales apart from
the south-east.

Like many another prudent Welsh ruler he considered it diplomatic
to maintain good relations with his English neighbours, pledging
homage to Athelstan, king of Wessex, in about 926, a strategy which
certainly did not endear him to the author of one of the great medieval
Welsh poems, '*Armes Prydain*' (930), a bitter diatribe against the
English. Nevertheless, Hywel was something of an Anglophile (he
named one of his sons Edwin) and was a particular admirer of Alfred
the Great. It is probable, therefore, that Hywel's main purpose in
making a pilgrimage to Rome in 928 was to emulate his hero who had
done the same thing many years before.

The achievement that was to earn Hywel the posthumous title of
'The Good' was his initiative in codifying, for the first time, the Laws of
Wales. Admiration of Alfred's own legal reforms, frustration with the

hotch-potch of tribal laws and customs operating within the Welsh lands now under his control, an undoubted vision of the essential unity of Wales (he issued his own silver pennies inscribed *Howael Rex*, the first Welsh ruler to do so), were all factors in his decision. Tradition has it that he summoned an assembly of the great and good of Wales, six men from every district, to Whitland in the 940s and told them to review and to rationalise existing laws and practices and produce a code of law that would apply throughout the country.

Exactly what they produced is not known for the earliest version that still survives dates from the beginning of the thirteenth century and contains various additions made during the intervening period. Nevertheless, some thirty-five manuscripts still exist, in Latin and Welsh, which capture the essence of the project which Hywel initiated, and which describe a remarkably civilised legal system which applied throughout Wales during the Middle Ages. Probably the most important laws prescribed how land should be divided amongst all the sons on the death of the father, in contrast with the primogeniture system that applied in England. Other laws defined the property rights of women in a remarkably enlightened manner while yet others proposed rational methods of trying to prove guilt.

Apart from the Welsh language the Laws of Hywel Dda were the most important symbol of the essential unity of Wales during the Middle Ages.

GWENLLÏAN
(c. 1097–1136)

T J Llewelyn Prichard, in his book *The Heroines of Welsh History* (1854) devoted a long chapter to Gwenllïan though most of it actually dealt with the activities of her husband. Prichard admitted that "our discerning readers who are conversant with Welsh history will be aware how scanty are the notices of that princess until circumstances altered her position, and from the gentle wife of a hero she became herself a heroine – a change of character as disadvantageous to her as it proved fatal in the end, however admirable in the peculiarity of its features".

She was born in Anglesey around 1097, the daughter of Gruffudd ap Cynan, king of Gwynedd, and by the time of her marriage to Gruffydd ap Rhys, prince of Deheubarth, around 1116 she was said (according to Prichard) to be a "blooming beauty". They lived in Cantref Mawr, the area between Dinefwr and Caeo, according to Gerald of Wales "the safest of refuges because of the tangled density of the forests". By all accounts (certainly Prichard's) they were a devoted couple, "affection the most pure and tender, connubial love, was ever present", and the marriage produced four sons.

By 1135 the power of the native Welsh rulers in south Wales was at a low ebb. However, that December saw the death of King Henry I, triggering a period of anarchy in England and initiating what Sir John Lloyd called the "great revolution in Welsh affairs". Hywel ap Meredydd of Brycheiniog's great victory over the Normans near Llwchwr on New Year's Day, 1136, encouraged Gruffydd ap Rhys to think of bringing Deheubarth fully under his control and he went north to secure the armed support of his wife's brothers, leaving his wife and sons at home. Receiving news of a Norman counter-attack which would scupper her husband's plans, Gwenllïan put herself at the head of an army and, with two of her sons riding beside her, she marched "like a Second Queen of the Amazons" (Gerald of Wales) from Ystrad Tywi down the Gwendraeth valley.

The army set up camp beneath Mynydd y Garreg, about a mile and a half from Cydweli castle, the stronghold of Maurice de Londres, but before she could launch an attack Maurice, supported by a mixed force of Norman, English and Flemish warriors, overwhelmed her gallant army. Her son Morgan was killed and another, Maelgwyn, was captured. Gwenllïan, injured, was also captured and (in the words of T J Llywelyn Prichard), "dignified to the last, but pallid with exhaustion and suppressed agony, calmly resigned to whatever further ills the fortunes of war might assign her". She was promptly beheaded by her noble foes and the spot is still known as Maes Gwenllïan.

Inspired partly no doubt by Gwenllïan's heroism the Welsh forces achieved some outstanding successes against the Normans in the following years and she would have been particularly proud of the achievements of her youngest son, 'Yr Arglwydd Rhys'.

RHYS ap GRUFFUDD
(1132–1197)

Rhys ap Gruffudd, generally known as 'Yr Arglwydd Rhys' (The Lord Rhys), was the outstanding Welsh ruler of his day.

The youngest son of Gruffydd ap Rhys, prince of Deheubarth, and his Amazonian wife, Gwenllïan, who died fighting the Normans, Rhys ap Gruffudd became sole ruler of Deheubarth in 1155. During the next two decades he transformed a weak and vulnerable region into the premier principality in Wales. This achievement was due not only to the relative weakness of the other two principalities, Powys and (after the death of Owain Gwynedd in 1170) Gwynedd, but also to the Lord Rhys' outstanding qualities. A fine warrior, he was able to take on the armies of Henry II and the Marcher Lords and win, but he was an equally shrewd diplomat when the occasion demanded. In return for acknowledging token allegiance to the King, who was preoccupied with other matters of state, in 1172 the Lord Rhys was appointed Justiciar for South Wales and given a free hand to run Deheubarth as he wished.

Rhys governed his principality from two centres, Dinefwr castle, the formidable stronghold high above the Tywi valley (recently well restored by Cadw), and Cardigan castle, rebuilt by him in stone and mortar in 1171, demonstrating how well the Welsh could acquire the skills of the Normans. He introduced important reforms in the management of his lands and brought together the mass of Welsh legal documents into book form.

Above all, the Lord Rhys was a great Welsh patriot, steeped in the cultural traditions of Wales, and he was responsible for convening what is now recognised as Wales' first National Eisteddfod at Cardigan castle in 1176. Although the winner of the chair for music was a minstrel from Rhys' own household the poets of Gwynedd won the bardic chair, demonstrating the cultural and linguistic if not political unity of Wales. The 800th anniversary of this event was celebrated at the Cardigan National Eisteddfod of 1976.

Rhys was also a great benefactor of the Church, particularly its monastic tradition. He founded Talley abbey and was largely responsible for the establishment of Strata Florida, where his eldest son and other relations were later to be buried, but not him.

The last few years of Rhys' life were marred by family quarrels and conflicts with the Marcher Lords, released from the moderating influence of Henry II who had died in 1189. However, nothing could detract from the Lord Rhys' great achievements and it was fitting that he should be buried in St David's cathedral, the resting place of St David himself. Predictably, the supremacy of Deheubarth within Wales did not long survive his death and the centre of political gravity moved north.

GERALD of WALES
(1146?–1223)

Giraldus Cambrensis, Gerald of Wales, was one of the most remarkable products of medieval Wales. Scholar, churchman, traveller, writer and patriot, his greatest achievement was as the outstanding chronicler of Welsh life during the Middle Ages, demonstrating, vividly, the extent to which there was a distinct Welsh community at the end of the twelfth century.

In a real sense Gerald was a semi-detached observer. He was certainly one-quarter Welsh and proud of it. The great Lord Rhys was a first cousin once removed. His grandmother had been none other than that celebrated beauty, Nest of Deheubarth, lover of Henry I among several others, and known to History as the "Helen of Wales". However, he was also three-quarters Norman, being the son of William de Barri, lord of Manorbier in Pembrokeshire.

Family connections and his own talents ensured that he enjoyed a fairly successful career in the Church (though failing to become Bishop of St David's in the 1170s), leading to his appointment as a royal chaplain in the Court of Henry II in 1184, a position he held for ten years, pursuing various diplomatic and ceremonial duties. In 1188 he accompanied Archbishop Baldwin of Canterbury on a tour of Wales to recruit warriors for the Third Crusade. This tour provided the material for Gerald's most celebrated works, his *Journey through Wales* and *A Description of Wales* in which he portrayed his native land and its people with great perception, affection and candour. "The Welsh," he wrote, "are extreme in all they do; so that if you never meet anyone worse than a bad Welshman, you will never meet anyone better than a good one." When it came to singing, "unlike the folk of other regions the Welsh do not sing their traditional songs in unison, but in many parts, and in many modes and modulations". No people were more hospitable: "Everyone's home is open to all and there is no need for travellers even to ask for accommodation." In his *Description of Wales* he reported what Meic Stephens has called one of the classic statements of Welsh patriotism, a comment made to King Henry II by the old man of Pencader in 1163:

> This nation, O King, may now, as in future times, be harrassed, and in a great measure weakened and destroyed by your and other powers; but it can never be totally subdued through the wrath of man, unless the wrath of God shall concur. Nor do I think that any other nation than this of Wales, or any other language, whatever may hereafter come to pass, shall on the day of severe examination before the Supreme Judge, answer for this corner of the earth.

As he got older, resentful at his failure to gain what he considered proper recognition within the English Court ("Were Gerald not a Welshman he would be worthy of high honour" said Henry II once), Gerald became increasingly patriotic himself, and in 1198 launched a truly heroic bid to become Bishop of St David's and achieve the independence of the Welsh Church from Canterbury with himself as Archbishop. Despite visiting Rome three times to plead his case to Pope Innocent III he encountered implacable opposition from the English authorities (An independent Church? Where would it all end?), and he finally gave up his hopeless cause in 1203. He spent much of the rest of his life in Lincoln, a disappointed man, but after his death he was, reputedly, buried in St David's Cathedral.

LLYWELYN ap IORWERTH
(1173–1240)

Llywelyn ap Iorwerth, Llywelyn Fawr ('The Great'), was the most powerful of the medieval rulers of native Wales.

Probably born at Dolwyddelan in 1173, the grandson of Owain Gwynedd, Llywelyn succeeded in bringing the whole of Gwynedd under his control so that by 1199 he was calling himself 'prince of the whole of north Wales'. Benefiting from English weakness during the reign of King John, Llywelyn proceeded to extend the influence of Gwynedd by military force and by 1218 he had become the most powerful Welsh ruler since the Norman Conquest. Though the English were to regain some territory on the fringe of his empire a few years later this did not seriously undermine his dominance over native Wales until his death.

Llywelyn kept the various princelings and chieftains in order through military might but, on the whole, like the Lord Rhys before him, he chose to maintain good relations with the English Court and the Marcher lords through shrewd diplomacy. Even when royal power was at its weakest Llywelyn was always careful to acknowledge the ultimate overlordship of the King of England. Marriage ties undoubtedly helped. Llywelyn himself married the illegitimate daughter of King John, and he married off his daughters into the leading marcher families.

Llywelyn never intended to unify native Wales into a single political state. He preferred to preside over what was in effect a federation of territories, with their rulers pledging homage to him, and there is no doubt that he kept a close eye on their activities, intervening when they appeared to be acting against his interests. However, during Llywelyn's rule, Gwynedd itself began to develop many of the characteristics of an independent state, a centralised administration, the use of great seals and privy seals to validate Llywelyn's authority, a rudimentary civil service, legal reforms, improvements in the revenue-collecting arrangements and land reform. The construction of several major castles, still admired to this day, Dolwyddelan, Dolbadarn, Cricieth, Castell y Bere, was a formidable assertion of princely power and influence, demonstrating also the extent to which Welsh builders of the time were up to date with the latest military technology. Elegant stonework found at the ruined Castell y Bere, now in the National Museum of Wales, also provides clear evidence of the sophistication of Llywelyn's court.

Though undoubtedly worthy of the title, Llywelyn never called himself prince of Wales, preferring from 1230 the title 'prince of Aberffro and lord of Snowdon'. It was some time after his death that he became to be hailed as Llywelyn the Great. Contemporaries however had no doubt about his standing. On his death at Aberconwy in 1240 the Cistercian annalist of the abbey referred to Llywelyn as "that great Achilles the Second". His final resting place is no longer known though the stone sarcophagus said to have been his, may be seen in Gwydir chapel, Llanrwst.

LLYWELYN ap GRUFFUDD
(died 1282)

Within a few years of the death of Llywelyn Fawr the unity of Wales had as usual collapsed so that by 1246 the chronicler Matthew Paris could write that "Wales had been pulled down to nothing". Within ten years however a new leader would arise who would change all that.

Llywelyn ap Gruffudd, grandson of Llywelyn Fawr, emerging from a period of internecine struggle, established himself as sole ruler of Gwynedd in 1255 and over the next three years, through force of arms and personality, succeeded in establishing his control over most of the rest of Wales. In 1258 an assembly of Welsh magnates pledged homage to Llywelyn who, from that time, styled himself 'Prince of Wales'.

Llewelyn crucially secured his position in the Treaty of Montgomery in 1267 when Henry III also acknowledged him as 'Prince of Wales' to whom all the other Welsh lords should pay homage. This event, the first ever occasion on which an English king had formally conceded this title to a Welsh leader, was the high point in Llywelyn's career. For a few years, like his grandfather before him, Llywelyn headed the rudiments of a virtually independent state, with an effective civil service and a revenue-raising capacity sufficiently sophisticated to enable Llywelyn to pay the dues owed to Henry under the terms of the treaty.

Tensions remained, however, between Llewelyn and his disaffected brothers, between him and some of the Marcher Lords who were unwilling to accept his authority and, crucially, from 1272, between him and the new King of England Edward I, a much tougher proposition than Henry III. In the past shrewd Welsh rulers had sought an accommodation with the English kings of the day, but this was not Llywelyn's style. He refused both to attend Edward's coronation and to pay homage to him. To Edward's displeasure he built Dolforwyn castle near the English stronghold at Montgomery. He determined to marry the daughter of Simon de Montfort, Edward's former enemy. While Edward put a stop to that by having her imprisoned he had had enough insubordination from Llywelyn and invaded Wales at the end of 1276.

Though deserted by many of his fair weather supporters Llywelyn resolutely resisted for nearly a year until, exhausted, he was forced to submit to the Treaty of Aberconwy. This reduced the area of his authority to part of Gwynedd, leaving Edward to bring most of the rest of Wales to heel during the following months. Inevitably, in 1282, the flames of revolt against English colonial oppression broke out again, this time initiated by Llywelyn's brother, Dafydd, so often in the past a thorn in his side. On 11 December, Llywelyn, fighting near Builth, and temporarily detached from his army, was killed in a chance encounter with an English lancer, the probable spot at Cilmeri now marked by a memorial.

Once recognised, Llywelyn's head was sent first to Edward in north Wales and then to London where it was paraded through the streets. His body was buried by the Cistercians in Abbey Cwm Hir, the assumed location now marked by a modern stone slab. The death of Llywelyn, 'Llywelyn ein Llyw Olaf', ended the cause of Welsh independence for several generations. The Welsh bards were distraught:

> O God, why does not the sea cover the land?
> Why are we left to linger?

DAFYDD ap GWILYM
(c. 1320–c. 1370)

Sir Thomas Parry, in his authoritative *History of Welsh Literature,*
devoted one whole chapter to Dafydd ap Gwilym. Nobody else was
honoured in this way, underlining Parry's widely shared view that
Dafydd ap Gwilym was Wales' greatest ever poet.

Many of the details of his life remain a little obscure. It is not
known for certain exactly when and where he was born, or when he
died and where he was laid to rest. There is a good deal of
circumstantial evidence, some of it found in Dafydd's own poems,
which places the year of his birth around 1320 and the place Bro
Gynin, near Llanbadarn. Embedded in what remains of the original
masonry is a memorial plaque, unveiled by Sir Thomas Parry in 1977,
which commemorates in Welsh, English and French the birthplace of
"one of the great poets of medieval Europe".

Wherein did his greatness lie? Though fully conversant with the
traditional Welsh verse forms current at the time, Dafydd is recognised
as the perfector, if not inventor, of a new and versatile Welsh verse
form, as vibrant now as it was in the fourteenth century, the *cywydd,* a
poem comprised of rhyming couplets, each line consisting of seven
syllables. Coming from the leisured classes and living during a period of
relative stability, he was able to travel throughout Wales, thereby
broadening his mental horizons. Moreover, being of noble stock and
moving in courtly circles (particularly those of his uncle, Llywelyn ap
Gwilym, Constable of Newcastle Emlyn), he was able to absorb not
only the sights and sounds of Wales but also wider Anglo-French and
indeed classical influences . He claimed to be 'Ovid's man'

('*dyn Ofydd*'). That shrewd observer George Borrow dubbed him not only the Welsh Ovid but the Welsh Horace and the Welsh Martial too, so marvellous was Dafydd's ability to write "poems of wonderful power on almost every conceivable subject".

Gwilym's enduring greatness lies in his ability to express with memorable sensitivity, poignancy and humour, the eternal themes of the beauty of nature (notably his bird poems) and the pursuit of love with all its attendant frustrations, in such sprightly poems as '*Merched Llanbadarn*' (the Girls of Llanbadarn) and '*Trafferth mewn Tafarn*' (Trouble at the Inn). Whatever he wrote, whether sacred or profane, reflected his profound reverence for the Creator and all his works.

Although there is a tradition that locates his resting place at Talley abbey it is generally accepted that he was buried near a yew tree at Strata Florida abbey. It was there in 1951 that the Honourable Society of Cymmrodorion erected a memorial to Dafydd to commemorate the society's bicentenary. It must surely be indicative of the poet's inspirational influence on his countrymen down the ages that when a group of Welshmen, later to become the cultural elite of their time, established at Oxford in 1886 a society dedicated to the promotion of Welsh culture, they named it *Cymdeithas Dafydd ap Gwilym*.

OWAIN LAWGOCH
(c. 1330–1378)

Although Wales experienced a semblance of peace during the fourteenth century this did not mean that the Welsh had stopped fighting. Indeed, during the Hundred Years' War between England and France the Welsh were to be found fighting on both sides. The contribution of the Welsh archers to English success at the battles of Crecy and Poitiers is legendary.

Other Welshmen chose to support the French cause. The most outstanding of these was Owain ap Thomas ap Rhodri (he probably got the name Owain Lawgoch, 'Owain of the red hand', because of heavily freckled rather than bloody hands). Born in Surrey, the son of a country gentleman, he went to France as a boy and was brought up within the French Court. A formidable warrior he fought the English at Poitiers and led mercenary armies, full of disaffected Welshmen, around Europe. Such was his standing with the French king that he was given the title 'Captain General' in 1369.

Owain was not however just a Welshman looking for adventure or nursing a grievance. It is true that because of his activities on the side of the French his English and Welsh lands had been confiscated, but what motivated him was something rather special. He was no less a figure than the great nephew of Llywelyn ap Gruffudd, and the fact that he had lived in Wales for no more than a year of his life in no way diminished his firm conviction that he was destined to recover Wales from English rule.

It suited the king of France, himself at war with England, to give Owain's princely aspirations every encouragement. Owain's plan to invade Wales in December 1369 was thwarted by bad weather, though the king of England was sufficiently alarmed to have the defences of his Welsh castles strengthened. In May 1372, Owain, with the enthusiastic support of Charles V, was again ready to lead an expedition to "the Principalyte of Wales, whereof I am rightfull heyre". However, having taken Guernsey from the English, he was forced to redirect his energies to fighting the English forces back on the French mainland.

Owain was never again to launch another attack on Wales. Nevertheless, hailed by the Welsh prophets as '*Y Mab Darogan*', the 'Son of Destiny', and enjoying genuine support back in Wales, Owain was considered a serious threat by the English authorities who in 1377, on hearing rumours of a possible invasion, with Castillian assistance, resolved to have Owain eliminated. They hired John Lamb, a Scottish assassin, to carry out the task during the siege of Mortagne-sur-Mer in September 1378, for a fee of £20.

The last in line of the House of Gwynedd was buried at the church of St Leger amidst much anguish and he soon became a folk hero back home. The memory of *'Yvain de Galles'*, recorded by the chronicler Froissart, was greatly cherished in France and this contributed significantly to the fostering of warm relations between France and Owain Glyndŵr, some years later.

OWAIN GLYNDŴR
(1359?–1415?)

In a recent worldwide poll among politicians and academics on the
most influential figures of the last millennium Owain Glyndŵr was
ranked seventh, ahead of Galileo, Isaac Newton and Abraham Lincoln,
surely an astonishing accolade for a man of the late Middle Ages who
took the limelight for little more than a decade before disappearing into
the mists of history, his mission an apparent failure. However, what the
poll honours is a man who, against all odds, confronted injustice and,
through the force of his personality, gave his people an inspiring and
enduring vision of a free and independent land.

At the end of the fourteenth century Wales was ripe for revolt.
There was much malaise among the people, increasingly impoverished
by economic dislocation. There was widespread resentment, especially
among the landed gentry and churchmen, at being treated as second
class citizens in their own country. This sentiment was fuelled by
influential bards, the custodians of the national heritage, who, in their
poetry, dwelled on the great years of the past and prophesied the great
years to come, when a messiah would emerge to lead his people
to freedom.

Owain Glyndŵr, born probably in 1359 at Sycharth in the Berwyn
hills, was to be that messiah. Though a prosperous landowner with
strong connections with English society, he fully shared the frustrations
of his countrymen, aggravated in 1399/1400 by personal humiliations
inflicted upon him under the new, insensitive, regime of Henry IV.
Moreover, he could trace his ancestry through all the princely dynasties
of Wales and with the death of Owain Lawgoch, the last descendant of

the princes of Gwynedd, in 1378, he could, with some justification, claim to be the true inheritor of the title, Prince of Wales.

On 16 September 1400, at his home in Glyndyfrdwy, near Corwen, he was proclaimed Prince of Wales by his family and closest followers, thus beginning a popular uprising against English rule which would embrace the squirearchy, the ecclesiastics and the common people, in the words of a contemporary annalist, "all the Welsh nation except a few".

Highlights include Owain's great set-piece victories at Mynydd Hyddgen in 1401 and at Pilleth in 1402; the capture, in 1404, of Harlech castle, one of the great symbols of English domination, where he made his headquarters; and in the same year, a sign of supreme self-confidence, the convening of the first Welsh Parliament at Machynlleth. In 1406, in the celebrated Pennal letter addressed to his ally, the King of France, Owain set out his vision of an independent Wales, including an independent Church and two universities, one in the north and one in the south. By now however Wales' first and last truly national revolt was running out of steam. Aberystwyth and Harlech castles fell in 1408/9 and by the end of the decade Owain Glyndŵr had become a guerrilla fighter, hunted, but never betrayed as long as he lived.

When and where he died is not known; probably in 1415, possibly at his daughter's home at Monnington Straddel, Herefordshire. In truth, Owain Glyndŵr, hailed as "the father of modern Welsh nationalism" by the great historian Sir John Lloyd, remains immortal.

CATRIN o FERAIN
(1534/5–1591)

If we discount Queen Elizabeth I, once famously called that "red-headed Welsh harridan" by the historian A L Rowse, Catrin o Ferain was surely the most celebrated Welsh woman of the sixteenth century. Indeed, as the daughter of Tudur ap Robert Vychan of Berain in Denbighshire, she had royal blood running through her veins, being the grand-daughter of an illegitimate son of Henry VII. Better still, according to her genealogist, William Cynwal of Penmachno, Catrin could trace her descent via generations of Welsh chieftains to Brutus, a great grandson of the Trojan hero Aeneas who, it was claimed, had settled in Wales, and, further back still, to the gods Jupiter and Saturn themselves. She was alleged, by the idle gossipers of the day, to have had a string of lovers, whom, once used, she disposed of one by one by pouring molten lead into their ears, before burying them in the orchard of her estate.

The best-known story about her is told by Thomas Pennant in his book *A Tour of Wales*. According to him, on the occasion of the funeral of Catrin's first husband, Sir John Salusbury, in 1566, she was forced to decline a proposal of marriage from Maurice Wynn of Gwydir because she had only just accepted a proposal from Sir Richard Clough on the way into the church. However, "she assured him that, in case she performed the same sad duty to the knight, he might depend on being the third". Within a few years Sir Richard Clough, one of the wealthiest men in Britain and the first in Wales to have a brick-built house since the time of the Romans, was dead and, true to her word, Maurice Wynn did indeed become her third husband. After his death in 1580

Catrin married her fourth and last husband, Edward Thelwall, the father of her daughter's husband.

Catrin experienced mixed fortunes during her later years. Her greatest tragedy was undoubtedly the execution of her eldest son, Thomas Salusbury, in 1586, for complicity in a plot to put Mary Queen of Scots on the throne of England, a loss she bore with much stoicism though her estates were threatened for a time. It was rumoured that Edward Thelwall kept her under a tight rein and mistreated her though there is no evidence for this. In fact when she died, at the age of fifty-six, the leading poets of the day eulogised her as a fine and generous lady.

Because of her several marriages to some of the leading members of Welsh society, compounded by the marriages of some of her own children to some of her step-children, which created a highly complex network of family relationships, Catrin came to be known as '*Mam Cymru*', the mother of Wales. Among her celebrated descendants were the Williams-Wynn dynasty of Wynnstay, and Hester Lynch Salusbury, wife of Henry Thrale and companion of Samuel Johnson.

WILLIAM MORGAN
(1545–1604)

In the view of many William Morgan was the most important Welshman of the last millennium. Born at Tŷ Mawr, Wybrnant, Penmachno (now owned by the National Trust), William Morgan studied at Cambridge from 1565 to 1571, during which time he was ordained as a deacon in the Church of England. In 1578 he became vicar at Llanrhaeadr-ym-Mochnant, Denbighshire, and while he was there he translated the whole of the Bible into Welsh, which was first published in 1588.

Although the great Welsh scholar William Salesbury and Richard Davies, bishop of St David's, had collaborated in the translation of the New Testament into Welsh in the 1560s they quarrelled and got no further and it fell to William Morgan to translate the Old and New Testaments and the Apocrypha into Welsh for the first time. This great achievement brought Morgan immediate fame and, together with his reputation as an accomplished preacher (something of a rarity in those days), led to his appointment first as bishop of Llandaff in 1595, and then as bishop of St Asaph in 1601. The latter move doubled his income which was just as well as he paid for the reroofing of the cathedral out of his own pocket. At his death he was buried in St Asaph's Cathedral, probably in the presbytery near to the bishop's throne though the exact spot is no longer known, the stone covering his grave having been moved during nineteenth century restoration work.

Through his translation of the Bible into a pure, classical Welsh, at a time when the language was at risk of degenerating into several crude dialects, William Morgan, more than any other single person, is credited with the preservation of the Welsh language. A uniform standard of Welsh was set, to be emulated by prose writers throughout the land, thereby, in the words of one Welsh scholar, "deepening Welshmen's consciousness of belonging together as a nation". He may also have ensured that Wales, now in possession of a Welsh Bible to be used to preach the Word of God, would remain in the Protestant tradition rather than go the way of the Irish. Certainly the four-hundredth anniversary of the translation of the Bible into Welsh was considered sufficiently important for the Post Office to issue a set of attractive commemorative postage stamps in 1988.

JOHN PENRY
(1563–1593)

John Penry has been called the first Welsh puritan martyr. He was undoubtedly a thorn in the flesh of Elizabethan England.

The Elizabethan religious settlement was essentially a compromise aiming to establish a middle ground between the extremes of Catholicism and Protestantism and, like most compromises, it did not suit everybody. It certainly did not impress John Penry. Born near Llangammarch Wells, Breconshire, he was educated at Oxford and Cambridge, where he became a puritan. From that standpoint he proceeded, in 1587 and 1588, to lambast the Government and Parliament with three celebrated treatises which condemned the dismal condition of religious life in his native land. In these treatises, which provide illuminating insights into the social life of contemporary Wales, he referred to his compatriots as "reprobates and castaways, aliens from the communion of the true Church, without all hope of the power of God to salvation, which is the Gospel". In the most insulting terms (he called the Welsh bishops "excrements of romish vomits") he blamed a neglectful and corrupt Church of England for this calamitous state of affairs. What Wales needed was an army of preaching ministers to proclaim the Gospel, not the "dumb ministers" already there and, if a sufficient number of ministers could not be found to preach the Gospel, using a Welsh-language Bible, then laymen should take on the task.

It is likely that Penry's strictures speeded up the appearance of William Morgan's Welsh Bible, but the vehemence of his attacks on the English establishment was not appreciated. Though some of his writings were exaggerated and unfair (George Owen of Henllys certainly thought so as far as his beloved Pembrokeshire was concerned) there was sufficient truth in his criticisms for him to be regarded as a dangerous man. Penry did not live in Wales during his short adult life, and he had little or no influence on the Wales of his day, but his writings struck a chord with Puritans in England and he became associated with a group of zealots who produced the so-called Marprelate Tracts, a series of highly scurrilous attacks on the leading lights of the Church of England.

For three years Penry escaped the clutches of the English authorities by fleeing to Scotland but on his return to London, where he joined the separatists, the most radical of puritan groups, he was arrested, found guilty of spurious offences against the Act of Uniformity and hanged in May 1593. He was thirty years old. He seems to have prophesied this outcome in his first treatise "*The Aequity of an Humble Submission*" in which, addressing the people of Wales, he had written: "I labour that you may have the Gospel preached among you. Though it cost me my life think it well bestowed."

Apart from his wife and four children, Deliverance, Comfort, Safety and Sure Hope, John Penry was mourned by few at the time though his principled, if often lonely, stand against the forces of the Establishment was to prove inspirational to later generations and he deserves respect as a sincere and courageous Welshman.

SAINT DAVID LEWIS
(1616–1679)

Saint David Lewis was the last Welsh Catholic martyr.

He was born in Abergavenny and he received an excellent education at the local grammar school where his father was the headmaster. After a smattering of legal training he visited Paris where he was converted to Roman Catholicism at the age of nineteen and in 1838 he went to Rome to train for the priesthood. In 1645, three years after ordination, he joined the Jesuits and in 1648 was sent to his native Monmouthshire to minister to his co-religionists. For thirty years, despite chronic bouts of toothache, he served the recusant community, rich and poor alike, with great devotion and no little courage, and was widely known as '*tad y tlodion*' ('father of the poor'), preaching to large congregations in both Welsh and English.

Though often denounced he retained his liberty until 1678. In that year England and Wales were swept by anti-Catholic hysteria when a Popish plot was alleged whereby King Charles II would be deposed by James, Duke of York, heir to the throne, who would be guided in his future policies by the Jesuits.

According to the master plan as revealed by Titus Oates, David Lewis would become Bishop of Llandaff.

In Monmouthshire, the priest-hunting was led by John Arnold of Llanfihangel Crucorney, a rabidly anti-Catholic member of parliament who, with others, arrested Lewis in November 1678. After several months' imprisonment in Monmouth and Usk gaols, during which time all attempts to link him with the Popish plot failed, Lewis was tried for being a priest in foreign orders before the Monmouthshire Assizes at Usk in March, 1679. Found guilty he was taken to London where he was offered, and refused, a reprieve from execution in return for information about the Popish plot and conformity to the Established Church. "Discover a Popish plot I could not, because I knew of none. Conform I would not because against my Conscience it was."

David Lewis was thereupon returned to Usk where, on 27 August 1679, after delivering a passionate sermon in Welsh and English, he was hanged on a rickety scaffold by the local blacksmith (others having refused to perform the task). He was buried in the churchyard of the Priory church, Usk, near to the west door. His gravestone is now worn smooth and next to it a new stone has been laid, recording that David Lewis, beatified in 1929, was one of forty English and Welsh Catholic martyrs canonised by Pope Paul VI in October 1970. Two relics are reportedly kept at the local Catholic church, a piece of the rope used to hang Lewis and some linen stained with his blood.

EDWARD LHUYD
(1660–1709)

In the Sir John Rhys Memorial Lecture of 1929 Sir Mortimer Wheeler hailed Edward Lhuyd as "our first Welsh Ancient Monuments Commission. He was the father both of field archaeology and philology in Wales; a worthy member of that generation of greats which included Newton and Wren. He worked with a perspicacity far in advance of that of most of his contemporaries and successors."

Edward Lhuyd (he also spellt his name Lloyd and Llwyd) was born in humble circumstances, an illegitimate child, but was fortunate to receive a sufficiently good education at Oswestry grammar school to enable him to enter Jesus College, Oxford, in 1682 where he prospered. His brilliant mind embraced all the main scientific enthusiasms of his day and, appointed underkeeper of the Ashmolean Museum in 1687 he became its head in 1691, a position he retained until his death. During this period he systematically classified the museum's holdings, starting with the fossil collection, and became, according to Sir Hans Sloane, "the best naturalist in Europe".

Lhuyd's central academic interest was in recording the rich history, culture and antiquities of the Celtic nations. However, this meticulous scholar was not content to develop his interest simply by sitting in his ivory tower in Oxford. He had nothing but contempt for those so-called experts who "never as much stooped in a gravel pit". For Lhuyd the only rational way to pursue his studies was to devise questionnaires, get out into the field, see the evidence, talk to the people. He spent several years travelling around the Celtic regions of Britain and beyond, not only Wales (where he visited every county), but also Scotland,

Ireland, Brittany and Cornwall, inspecting ancient sites, collecting manuscripts, fossils and all sorts of other artifacts. So unusual was his approach that he initially encountered widespread suspicion wherever he went; in Pembrokeshire he was thought to be a magician; in Brittany he was briefly detained as a spy.

In 1707 he published some of the results of his research in the monumental *Archaeologica Britannica: an Account of the Languages, Histories and Customs of Great Britain*, a work which is recognised as the beginning of the study of comparative philology. Elected a Fellow of the Royal Society in 1708, the most brilliant Welshman of his day died in his prime in the following year at the early age of forty-nine and was buried in the 'Welsh aisle' of St Michael's church, Oxford. Although he died too soon his pioneering work laid the foundations for the renaissance in Welsh culture that took place during the eighteenth century. In the words of Sir John Rhys, himself the outstanding Celtic scholar at the beginning of the twentieth century, Edward Lhuyd was "a great man, a very great man".

GRIFFITH JONES
(1683–1761)

Griffith Jones was quite simply one of the greatest Welshmen of the eighteenth century. A Carmarthenshire man through and through he felt himself called by God to rid early eighteenth century Wales of its "miserable blindness" in spiritual terms and travelled the countryside preaching passionate hell-fire sermons wherever he could find open space and an audience. He would challenge his cringing listeners thus:

> Consider what it will be like to be boiled in a huge cauldron of God's wrath; what it will be like to burn in the unquenchable fire, in the fiery furnace, in the lake which burns with fire and brimstone.

A man of towering authority Jones was an inspiration to some of the greatest evangelists of the age and it was after hearing him preach that Daniel Rowland was converted in 1735.

Griffith Jones has an even greater claim to fame as the person who established the Circulating Schools movement in Wales in 1731. He was determined to make the Welsh people, especially the hitherto neglected poor and underpriveleged, literate. He recruited, and at his seminary, 'Yr Hen Goleg' at Llanddowror, carefully trained an army of itinerant teachers who toured Wales in order to help people, children and adults, to read, and at times of the day and periods of the year most convenient to the learners. In general they were taught in their own vernacular tongue which for most people was Welsh. Indeed Jones preferred them to learn in their native tongue as this would be less disruptive to local community life. Moreover, Jones never sought to provide a broadly-based education, including arithmetic or writing, attributes that he considered unnecessary for simple country folk. Rather they were taught to read primarily the Scriptures and other improving texts. In other words Jones, who in many ways had a very conservative outlook, regarded his movement very much as an instrument of social control, an aim which probably encouraged many self-interested philanthropists to offer financial support.

His greatest patron was Madam Bridget Bevan, a wealthy and pious heiress who lived in Laugharne and who, after Jones' death in 1761, continued to promote his movement and who, on her own death in 1779, was buried alongside Jones in the chancel of Llanddowror church.

It is estimated that the circulating schools movement brought literacy of sorts to about half the population of Wales, and came to the notice of people as far away as Catherine the Great of Russia. It secured the vitality of the Welsh language and because of its particular focus, contributed to the revival of the Christian faith during the second half of the century.

Not a bad legacy, all in all.

GRIFFITH MORGAN
(Guto Nyth-brân) (1700–1737)

If the accounts are true (and why not?) Griffith Morgan, universally
known as Guto Nyth-brân, must have been the greatest runner of
all time.

Born at Llwyncelyn, Guto, a shepherd, lived at Nyth-brân farm in
the hills above Mountain Ash. He is reputed to have developed his
running skills by herding recalcitrant sheep, and he quickly established a
reputation as the fleetest runner in Wales. Some of his feats are
legendary, such as the time he beat a horse over a one mile race in
Carmarthen and it is said that he once ran from his home to Pontypridd
and back to fetch an errand for his mother before her breakfast kettle
had boiled, a remarkable achievement indeed. Guto is reputed to have
run fifty yards in four seconds and ten miles in forty-five minutes. His
unique method of training involved lying up to his neck in farmyard
manure twice a week, a practice which, he claimed, made his muscles
and tendons supple.

Perhaps not surprisingly he never married but he had a long-term
relationship with his girl-friend, 'Siân o' Siop', who was also his
manager. She was to play a key role in the most celebrated event in
Guto's life, which is recorded on his gravestone next to the door of St
Gwynno's church, Llanwynno. On 6 September 1737 he ran a twelve
mile race against an opponent known as 'the Prince' from Newport to
Bedwas church, defeating him easily in the astonishing time of fifty
three minutes. Arriving at the winning post, having evaded all attempts
by saboteurs to slow him down, Guto was enthusiastically greeted by
Siân, who had bet a substantial sum on the outcome. "*Da iawn Guto,*

da iawn," ("Well done") she squealed, slapping him firmly on the back, a gesture which caused him to drop down dead, uttering, according to some accounts, the words *"Dyna ti wedi fy lladd i!"* ("There, you have killed me!")

Guto's statue stands in the main square of Mountain Ash and, since 1958, his achievement has been commemorated (with a break of some years) in the Nos Galan races held in Mountain Ash, with a mystery celebrity runner, representing the spirit of Guto Nyth-brân, running from Guto's grave to the town below, carrying a flare.

THE MORRIS BROTHERS OF ANGLESEY

The Morris brothers of Anglesey (*Morisiaid Môn*) were among the most remarkable families of eighteenth century Wales.

The best known, and ablest, of them was Lewis Morris (1701–1765) who could turn his hand to almost anything. The son of an Anglesey carpenter, he became a surveyor of taxes in his native county and learnt to be a land surveyor so that in 1746 he was appointed sub-steward of Crown lands in Cardiganshire. Although this job got him into all sorts of difficulties with the local squirearchy he managed to devote such free time as he had to a whole range of other pursuits, from farming through cartography to watch-making.

His greatest accomplishments were in the cultural arena. A fervent patriot, he was determined to defend the literary heritage and language of Wales in the face of encroaching Anglicisation. He strove to preserve Welsh poetry and set up his own printing press which he used to publish, in 1735, an anthology of Welsh classical poetry under the title *Tlysau yr Hen Oesoedd* (Treasures of Ancient Times). He was no mean poet himself, but his greatest contribution to Welsh culture was as an assiduous patron of other leading literary figures of the time, including the celebrated poet Goronwy Owen, Evan Evans (Ieuan Fardd), the frustrated curate regarded by Sir Thomas Parry as the greatest Welsh scholar of the century, Thomas Pennant, the antiquarian, traveller and much else, and Thomas Richards, the man who produced a pioneering Welsh-English dictionary.

If Lewis Morris was the hub of the so-called 'Morris Circle' of Welsh scholars and poets his brother Richard (1703–1779) was an important influence too. He was the one with the organisational flair and, a civil servant living in London for all his adult life, he was primarily responsible for the establishment of the Honourable Society of Cymmrodorion in 1751. He and Lewis intended the society to become an influential hotbed of Welsh language and learning in the capital city though it more often served as a club where the leading lights of London Welsh society could socialise and gossip. However, the society did serve as the launching-pad, a generation later, of the Gwyneddigion Society, an important landmark in the development of Welsh culture.

A third brother, William (1705–1763), yet another civil servant and a noted botanist, remained in Anglesey all his life, and he wrote to his brothers constantly. Indeed, one of the greatest literary contributions of the Morris brothers was the voluminous correspondence, still preserved, that they conducted with each other and with members of the wider Morris Circle, which provides a unique insight into Welsh life in the eighteenth century.

The great literary critic, Professor W J Gruffudd, once wrote of the Morris brothers: "Had these three not thought their thoughts, had they not done their work and lived as they did, it is quite certain that the nineteenth century would have been very different from what it was, and that Welsh literature today would have been much the poorer."

RICHARD WILSON
(1713–1782)

Richard Wilson is universally acknowledged as the father of British landscape painting.

He was born in Penegoes near Machynlleth where his father was the local rector and in 1729 he was sent to London where he became apprenticed to Thomas Wright, a portrait painter. Although by the 1740s he was sufficiently talented to have established himself as one of the leading portrait painters in London he did not possess an immediately endearing personality. One contemporary described Wilson as "rough to the taste at first, tolerable by a little longer acquaintance" and by the time he left for Italy in 1750 his preference for painting places rather than people was already evident.

It was during his seven years in Italy, mainly in and around Rome, that Wilson became totally committed to landscape painting, abandoning portraiture for ever, or at least human portraiture, for on his return to London he became established as the leading exponent of what was called the 'country house portrait', his series of paintings of Wilton House, Wiltshire, being generally regarded as the greatest of his time. Richard Wilson is, however, especially remembered for his scenes of Wales, "the cream of his work" according to Ellis Waterhouse, the distinguished art historian, producing particularly striking paintings of Snowdon, Cadair Idris, Cilgerran and Caernarfon castles and of Dinas Brân from Llangollen. One of his best-known works (undertaken, it is said, to clear a debt) was the sign which used to be outside the Loggerheads Inn on the Mold-Ruthin road, though it seems now to have disappeared. Named 'We three loggerheads' (blockheads), only two heads were depicted, the third being that of the observer.

Wilson became a founding member of the Royal Academy in 1760. Always short of money his appointment as its librarian in 1776 at an annual salary of £60 helped to keep body and soul together for a time but, increasingly overwhelmed by ill-health and drunken poverty, he spent his last months at Colomendy Hall, near Mold, the home of a relative. After his death he was buried in Mold parish churchyard, where his chest tomb can be seen near to the north wall of the church. Though dying in obscurity Wilson greatly influenced such masters as Constable and Turner. Indeed Turner made a pilgrimage to Wilson's birthplace in 1798 during his Welsh tour.

In 1983 the National Museum of Wales celebrated its 75th anniversary by hosting a major exhibition of the works of one of Wales' greatest artists.

HOWEL HARRIS
(1714–1773)

If Daniel Rowland was the orator of the Welsh Methodist revival of the eighteenth century and William Williams, Pantycelyn, the hymn writer, Howel Harris was the inspired organiser and, in the opinion of some, the greatest Welshman of his age.

Born near Talgarth, the school-teacher son of a prosperous farmer, Harris experienced a dramatic religious conversion in 1735. "I felt suddenly my heart melting within me, like wax before the fire, with love to God my Saviour." Thwarted in his ambition to become an ordained clergyman – he was thought to be far too enthusiastic a Christian – he journeyed Wales, preaching the Gospel, often to huge crowds. He organised his converts into local societies of Methodists and though he encountered some hostility, especially in north Wales where, in his view, the people had "poor, silly minds", by 1750 over 400 societies had been formed, the great majority in the counties of south Wales.

Harris was, however, arrogant and autocratic (some called him 'Pope Harris'). In 1750, because of doctrinal and personality differences with his leading colleagues, including Daniel Rowland, and somewhat discredited because of an apparently too close association with the unhappy wife of a drunken squire, he withdrew from the stage, retiring to his birthplace, Trefeca. Here in 1752 he set up a self-sufficient quasi-monastic community where he, 'Father', ruled his 'Family' with a rod of iron and pioneered some of the agricultural innovations of the period; he was one of the founders, in 1755, of the Brecknockshire Agricultural Society, the first of its kind in Wales.

He resumed active involvement in the Methodist movement in

1763 but the charismatic Daniel Rowland was now its acknowledged leader and Harris never regained his former prominence. However, it is said that over 20,000 people attended his funeral in 1773 and the commemorative tablet marking his burial place near the communion table in Talgarth parish church harks back to the time of his conversion in 1735:

> Here where his body lies, he was convinced of sin, had his pardon sealed, felt the power of Christ's precious blood at Holy Communion.

WILLIAM WILLIAMS
(Pantycelyn) (1716–1791)

William Williams, Pantycelyn, is
Wales' greatest hymnwriter. Born in
Llandovery of farming stock,
William Williams' first ambition
was to become a doctor but,
inspired by the preaching of Howel
Harris, and failing in 1743 to
become ordained in the Church of
England because of his association
with the Methodists, he spent
the rest of his life advancing
the Methodist cause in
Wales.

   Though Williams was
a popular itinerant preacher
and first-class organiser of
Methodist societies, travelling
nearly 150,000 miles on horseback during his career, his greatest
contribution to the Methodist Revival was as a hymnwriter, indeed the
greatest of all hymnwriters. His output was prodigious, comprising over
nine hundred hymns, including such evergreens as "*Pererin wyf mewn
anial dir*" (sung to the tune 'Amazing Grace') and "*Guide me O thou
great Jehovah*" (sung to 'Cwm Rhondda'). He once attributed his poetic
gifts to:

...enjoyment of God, and experience, together with the force of heavenly fervour, boiling together within, until the fire breaks forth in sweet songs that shall endure for ever.

He is still widely referred to by Welsh preachers as *Y Pêr Ganiedydd* (The Sweet Singer). Elfed, next to Williams the most prolific of all Welsh hymnwriters, once said: "As Luther sang Germany into Protestantism so did Williams sing Wales of the eighteenth century into piety."

He was not only a prolific writer of hymns but of prose too, including *Ductor Nuptiarum* (1777), a marriage guide full of wisdom and commonsense. His own married life, at Pantycelyn, was fruitful, producing eight children.

He is buried at Llanfair-ar-y-bryn churchyard on the outskirts of Llandovery. On the substantial obelisk which marks his grave in the north-east of the churchyard is written:

He laboured in the service of the Gospel for near half a century and continued incessantly to promote it both by his Labours and Writings; and to his inexpressible Joy beheld its influence extending and its efficacy witnessed in the Conviction and conversion of many thousands.

RICHARD PRICE
(1723–1791)

Richard Price was a distinguished political scientist whose writings
inspired two revolutions. Indeed, the historian John Davies considers
Price to be the most original thinker ever born in Wales.

A cousin of Ann Maddocks, 'the Maid of Cefn Ydfa', Richard Price
was born the son of a Dissenting minister in Tyn-ton, a farmhouse in
the parish of Llangeinor, Glamorgan, and was educated at various
schools in Neath, Carmarthen and Talgarth. Following the deaths of his
father and mother in quick succession he completed his education in
London and there he remained for much of the rest of his life, serving as
a minister to a presbyterian congregation in Stoke Newington for nearly
thirty years. He remained sufficiently in touch with his roots however to
become Grand Master of the Bridgend Lodge of Freemasons in 1777.

By the age of thirty-five he had seen the publication of his first
influential work, *A Review of the Principal Questions and Difficulties in
Morals,* in which he anticipated and challenged John Stuart Mill's later
doctrine of Utilitarianism whereby Right or Wrong would be
determined by the extent to which an action did good to most people.
As far as Price was concerned Right and Wrong were absolute concepts
which could not be defined in such equivocal terms.

Holding such purist views it is hardly surprising that he came out
strongly in favour of American self-determination in the 1770s. In his
pamphlet *Observations on the Nature of Civil Liberty* (1776) he argued
that sovereignty rested with the people, that kings and ministers were
servants, and not the masters of the people. His arguments had such an
impact in America that in 1778 the American Congress resolved that:

It is the Desire of Congress to consider him as a Citizen of the United States, and to receive his Assistance in regulating Their Finances.

Though flattered (he was not only a philosopher but a pioneer of actuarial science who trained his nephew William Morgan of Bridgend to become the greatest actuary of his time), he declined the offers but accepted, with George Washington, the honorary degree of LL.D from Yale University in 1781.

Price's views about the right of people to self determination (Mirabeau translated his pamphlet into French) meant that he inevitably welcomed the outbreak of the French Revolution, expressing his support in a famous sermon *A Discourse on the Love of our Country* (1789), in which he defined patriotism as the search for freedom and justice. This stance led Edmund Burke to produce his rejoinder, *Reflections on the Revolution in France* (1790). It is recorded that when Price died in 1791 the French Assembly went into mourning.

EDWARD WILLIAMS
(Iolo Morganwg) (1747–1826)

Together the Gorsedd of Bards and the National Eisteddfod represent
the most powerful affirmation of the continuing strength of the
language and culture of Wales. One man deserves the credit for
establishing this celebration, that flawed genius Edward Williams,
universally known by his bardic name Iolo Morganwg.

Iolo was born in the Vale of Glamorgan, the son of a stonemason, a
trade he would himself take up with some skill (examples of his work
can be seen in St Mary's Church near Cowbridge). Though largely self-
educated he was fortunate to come under the influence of some of the
leading scholars of an area vibrant with new radical thinking. He
developed a passionate interest in poetry and antiquarianism,
strengthened during those periods when he worked in and around
London, associating with some of the leading lights of London Welsh
society in the Gwyneddigion Society.

There was a strong determination among Welsh scholars of the late
eighteenth century to revive an interest in and appreciation of Welsh life
and culture and Iolo soon found himself at the centre of this movement.
Indeed, his mind unbalanced by a chronic addiction to drugs, Iolo
became obsessed with his mission to demonstrate the unique richness of
the Welsh heritage, particularly whatever emanated from his beloved
county of Glamorgan. Wandering through south Wales with a satchel
on his back, from library to library, he assembled a substantial archive in
order to extol the history and traditions of his native land and,
influenced by heavy doses of laudanum, where the evidence was lacking
he made it up so that for years afterwards it was unclear what was true

and what was false. His brilliance was such that for decades verses composed by him were attributed to Dafydd ap Gwilym and scholars were furious for having been fooled. He may have fooled them but not his long-suffering wife who once wrote: "Dear Ned, you are still building castles in the air which will crush you under their ruins."

Many of his finest fabrications dealt with his conviction that Wales was the home of bardic traditions going back to the time of the Druids. Seeking to reconnect the Welsh with their glorious past, he assembled the first Gorsedd of Bards on Primrose Hill in 1792 (he was living in London at the time), involving a circle of stones and the ritual sheathing of swords, and three years later, retreating from a city which regarded him as a subversive radical, convened the first Welsh Gorsedd on Stalling Down, near Cowbridge. Finally, in 1819, at an eisteddfod sponsored by the Cambrian Society of Dyfed, held at the Ivy Bush Inn, Carmarthen, Iolo achieved his aim to link his Gorsedd of Bards, and its attendant ceremonial, to the eisteddfod movement, hitherto a rather low key and provincial affair, turning the occasion into a dramatic expression of Welsh culture. Though some disapproved of the ungodly presence of the harp the event set the pattern for the National Eisteddfodau of future years. Indeed, Professor G J Williams, who later did much to expose Iolo's weaknesses, acknowledged that "Iolo gave to Wales a national institution" and "a cultural focus to the nation".

In Flemingston church, Glamorgan, where Iolo lies, a memorial carries a fulsome tribute to one of Wales' most fertile minds.

JEMIMA NICHOLAS
(1750–1832)

Until recently visitors to St Mary's church hall in Fishguard would have been able to see Wales' version of the Bayeux Tapestry, a hundred-foot long tapestry produced by seventy local stitchers, depicting the main events of the last invasion of Britain in 1797. One of the most striking sections showed the formidable Jemima Nicholas holding a pitchfork in one hand and a cowering French soldier in the other, and surrounded by other miserable-looking French captives.

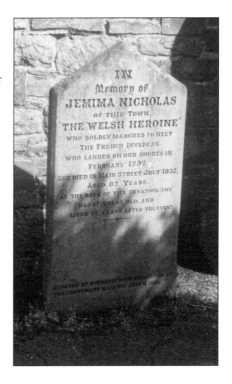

In February 1797 a French army of some 1,400 men landed near Fishguard, the intention being to provide a diversion while the main French forces invaded Ireland. Most of the troops were convicts, "a gaggle of criminals led by a paranoid American" to use Gwyn A Williams' colourful description. The assault was a total disaster and on the third day the French, drunk and demoralised, surrendered to Lord

Cawdor, captain of the Castlemartin Yeomanry, on Goodwick sands.

One of the incidents during this short-lived war involved Jemima Nicholas, the local cobbler, said to be an Amazonian six-foot tall and fearsome to behold. It is recorded that she made her way to Llanwnda, armed with a pitchfork, and single-handedly rounded up twelve Frenchmen in a field and brought them back to town. It is said that she then went off to look for more but whether she found any is not known; they may have wisely run for cover.

This incident made Jemima into a local celebrity, and as a reward the British government paid her a pension of fifty pounds a year for the rest of her life. On her death in 1832 the vicar of Fishguard wrote the following in the parish register:

> The woman was called Jemima Vawr, ie the Great, from her heroic acts, she having marched against the French who landed hereabout in 1797, and being of such personal powers as to be able to overcome most men in a fight. I recollect her well.

Though she never married she is said to have had a daughter, Eliza, and possibly also a son.

Exactly where Jemima lies in St Mary's churchyard, Fishguard, is no longer known but near to the church door stands a memorial stone to: "The Welsh heroine who boldly marched to meet the French invaders who landed on our shores in February 1797".

THOMAS CHARLES
(1755–1814)

Thomas Charles was a pioneer of the Sunday School movement in Wales. Born and brought up in Carmarthenshire, after a spell as an Anglican curate in Somerset, in 1783 he settled in Bala, the home town of his wife, who was not prepared to leave her shop (which provided a useful income in later years). He quickly became the major force in the spread of Methodism in north Wales, ultimately leading to the historic split with the Anglican church in 1811, a development in which he was centrally involved, though initially with some reluctance.

Thomas Charles was a superb organiser and preacher. His greatest achievement, building on the circulating schools legacy of Griffith Jones, was to pioneer, from about 1789, the Sunday School movement in Wales, the distinctive feature of which was its appeal not only to children but also to adults from all walks of life, thereby, it has been argued, contributing to the development of the democratic culture considered characteristic of Welsh life in the decades that followed.

The Sunday Schools created a demand for Bibles which resulted in Thomas Charles and others founding the British and Foreign Bible Society in 1804, one of its first projects being the publication of twenty thousand copies of a new version of the Welsh Bible produced by Thomas Charles. He also published a biblical dictionary in four volumes, *Y Geiriadur Ysgrythyrawl* (1805–11) and a guide to the principles of the Christian Faith, *Hyfforddwr yn Egwyddorion y Grefydd Gristnogol* (1807) to assist readers of the Bible in their studies. The bible shortage had most forcefully been drawn to his personal attention in 1800 by a sixteen-year-old girl, Mary Jones (1784–1864). A Welsh heroine in her own right, Mary, having saved up her pennies, had walked from her home in Llanfihangel-y-Pennant to Bala, a journey of twenty-five miles, in order to buy a bible from Thomas Charles. Not having one to sell, and impressed by Mary's piety, he gave her his own copy. His house in Bala, now the site of Barclay's bank, bears a plaque to commemorate this event. After Mary's death the British and Foreign Bible Society acquired her treasured Bible, which is now preserved in the library of the University of Cambridge.

After his death Thomas Charles was buried in Llanycil churchyard, near Bala.

David Charles (1762–1834), Thomas' brother, was the author of three of Wales' greatest hymns, *O! Iesu Mawr, O fryniau Caersalem* and *Rhagluniaeth fawr y nef*, usually sung, respectively, to the hymn-tunes 'Llef', 'Crug-y-bar' and 'Builth'.

ROBERT OWEN
(1771–1858)

"If I were asked who was the greatest Welshman during the reign of Victoria, I would answer without hesitation, Robert Owen of Newtown and New Harmony, the apostle of labour." So wrote Owen M Edwards in 1897.

Born in Newtown, the son of a saddler and ironmonger, Robert Owen is acknowledged as the pioneer of utopian socialism in Britain. After leaving Montgomeryshire at the age of ten he learnt the drapery trade in Lincolnshire and London before going to Manchester where he prospered in the cotton-spinning business. Moving to Scotland in 1799 he established at New Lanark a model factory run on the premise that one could treat the workforce properly and still make a profit.

He was a rationalist, having no time for organised religion, who believed that human nature was the product of human society, that cooperation was better than competition and that mankind could change for the better through social and moral education. Such doctrines, best expressed in his influential work *A New View of Society or Essays on the Formation of Human Character* (1813) were inevitably unpalatable to the ruling classes of the time who preferred the masses to be kept in their place. Owen's efforts to establish trade unionism in the 1820s and 1830s collapsed, ultimately leading to the deportation of the unfortunate 'Tolpuddle Martyrs' to Australia. Owen's beliefs were embraced with greater success in the following decade when twenty-eight men, the 'Rochdale Pioneers', established the Co-operative Movement in 1844, proclaiming the idea of progress through self-help, a concept more in tune with the times.

During his later years Owen spent some time in America and visited France. He considered standing for Parliament and, rather surprisingly, dabbled in Spiritualism, making apparent contact with the likes of Benjamin Franklin and Thomas Jefferson, reporting that they were both "very happy". He returned to Newtown to die in 1858, suffering the indignity of a Christian funeral.

Owen's elegant grave in old St Mary's churchyard was given its present appearance in 1902 when elaborate wrought iron railings, erected by the Co-operative Union, were unveiled by the veteran radical George Jacob Holyoake. A more recent memorial was unveiled by Ann Clwyd MP in 1993. One of the railings carries a statement of Owen's which encapsulates his philosophy:

> It is the one great and universal interest of the human race to be cordially united and to aid each other to the full extent of their capacities.

It is therefore hardly surprising that Owen M Edwards held his compatriot in such high regard. So did others. A bust of Robert Owen, sculpted by Sir William Goscombe John, was presented as a gift from the Welsh people to the International Labour Office when it was established in Geneva.

ANN GRIFFITHS
(1776–1805)

Ann Griffiths, born Ann Thomas, a farmer's daughter, lived all of her
life at Dolwar Fach, deep in the Montgomeryshire countryside, and
died before the age of thirty, shortly after giving birth to her only child
(who also died). She is, however, generally ranked with William
Williams, Pantycelyn, as among the greatest of Welsh religious poets.

Though by all accounts a lively and outgoing teenager, she lived in a
community imbued with the fervour of the Methodist Revival and,
having experienced a religious conversion in 1796, she spent the rest of
her life praising God. During this time this remarkable young woman,
who would have received little in the way of formal education (though
she knew her Bible backwards) composed nearly eighty poems (perhaps
more), many of which have become hymns of immense power,
revealing an overwhelming passion for the love of Christ. Probably her
best-known poem, 'Lo, between the myrtles standing', is often sung to
the tune 'Cwm Rhondda' and ends "O to rest me All my lifetime in
his love!"

Her writings are referred to here as poems because Ann Griffiths did
not intend them to be sung as hymns; had she done so the metre would
surely have been simpler. Indeed, she never kept a systematic record of
her output. Few, if any, of her poems would have survived if Ruth
Evans, an illiterate maidservant in the Griffiths household, had not
committed them to memory, later recalling them to her husband, John
Hughes of Pontrobert, an eminent preacher, who wrote them down.

Ann Griffiths' farmhouse home, Dolwar Fach, is still maintained as
a shrine to her memory. Her grave in Llanfihangel-yng-Ngwynfa

churchyard, near Llansilin, is marked by a substantial obelisk on the left-hand side of the path leading to the church.

At the nearby hamlet of Dolanog stands a Calvinistic Methodist chapel, Capel Coffa Ann Griffiths, which honours not only her memory but also Ruth Evans, the by no means simple domestic servant, but for whose astonishing power of recall few would ever have heard of the person described on a plaque as 'Prif Emynyddes Cymru' ('Wales' greatest woman hymnwriter').

SIR JOHN and
LADY CHARLOTTE GUEST

The contribution of this devoted couple to the social and economic life of nineteenth century Wales was impressive to say the least.

Born in Dowlais, where he lived for most of his life, Josiah John Guest (1785–1852) was the owner of the Dowlais Iron Company, the largest and most advanced ironworks in the world in the early nineteenth century. Awarded the FRS in 1830, he became a baronet in the Coronation Honours List of July 1838 and at the time of his death (leaving £500,000 in his will, a huge sum in those days) he was compared in the *Times* with such industrial giants as the Arkwrights and Peels. Between 1826 and 1830 he was a Canningite MP for Honiton and, having lost his seat, showing somewhat 'leftward' tendencies, he became the first MP for his home town of Merthyr Tydfil in 1832, holding the seat until his death.

Though a moderate Liberal in politics Guest moved from Wesleyanism to Anglicanism in religion and achieved his ambition to become a member of the landed gentry in the 1840s by acquiring a country estate at Canford, Dorset, enabling him to enter 'landed proprietor' as his occupation in the 1851 census. He died in 1852 after some years of ill-health and was buried in the now derelict St John's church which he had built in Dowlais in 1827. It is estimated that 20,000 mourners attended his funeral.

Sir John's second wife, Lady Charlotte Bertie (1812–1895), the daughter of the Ninth Earl of Lindsey, was a person of great distinction in her own right. Apart from giving birth to ten children between 1834 and 1847 she played a notable part in the life of the local community, particularly in the provision of an enlightened Prussian-style school system for the children of Dowlais, and for some years after her husband's death took over the running of the ironworks. A close friend of the redoubtable Lady Llanover, she immersed herself in the cultural affairs of "my own dear country" and, having painstakingly taught herself medieval Welsh under the guidance of the local rector, she proceeded, with some help, to translate and publish, for the first time, *The Mabinogion*, a collection of medieval Welsh tales of romance and chivalry drawn from the 14th century *Red Book of Hergest*. In the view of one 'Mabinogion' authority, "translation apart, the voluminous notes appended to each story bespeak a range of knowledge and a breadth of scholarship, English, Welsh and Continental, which mark her out as one of the most remarkable women of the Victorian age".

In 1855 she married her son's tutor, Charles Schreiber, and became an avid traveller and collector of fine china. By the time of her death, at Canford Manor, her south Wales days were well in the past and in its obituary the *Times* did not even mention her translation of *The Mabinogion*, the achievement for which she is still honoured in her adopted land.

BETI CADWALADR
(1789–1860)

Beti Cadwaladr, a heroine of the Crimean War, did not match the conventional nineteenth century profile of a dutiful Welsh wife and mother. Born and brought up near Bala, the daughter of a prominent local Methodist preacher and poet, she could not wait to leave home, at the age of fourteen, to see the world. She assumed the name Elizabeth Davies, 'Cadwaladr' being too much of a mouthful for the English to swallow. Most of the rest of her life was divided between working as a domestic servant, first in Liverpool, then in London and travelling the world on board a variety of ships, providing support for the captains and their families. In this way Beti visited Africa, Asia (she met the missionary William Carey in India), South America and Australia. She never married, though she had her chances, including a wealthy ninety-year-old Tasmanian ex-convict; R T Jenkins called her "a somewhat masculine woman".

For many years she lived with her sister in London and, when well into middle age, she trained as a nurse at Guy's Hospital, a career move which was to stand her in good stead a few years later. For after reading in the *Times* an account of the battle of the Alma in 1854, when British soldiers in their hundreds were dying of cholera, exposure and untreated wounds, this intrepid and selfless traveller, now aged sixty-five, resolved to go out to the Crimea to help.

Beti's initial posting at Scutari proved highly unsatisfactory. She did not take to Florence Nightingale. She later wrote in her autobiography: "I did not like the name Nightingale. When I first hear a name I am very apt to know by my feelings whether I shall like the person who bears it." Beti was quite unable to accept Florence's imperious discipline. After a few weeks Beti and a few other women moved on to Balaclava, there to encounter the most horrific conditions. She remained there for several months, nursing the sick soldiers with devotion, cutting through the red tape that hampered the distribution of supplies to the wounded soldiers and running the extra diet kitchen which catered for the most needy. From time to time Florence Nightingale would pay a visit, to be greeted with a degree of coolness. "I should as soon have expected to see the Queen here as you."

By October 1855 Beti's health, assaulted by constant deprivation, finally broke down and, not wishing to die in a foreign land, she reluctantly decided to return home, with the grateful thanks of those who remained behind ringing in her ears. One colleague paid a particularly handsome tribute to " this respectable and truly good woman, who has sacrificed her health, almost her life, for the good of her suffering countrymen".

In fact Beti lived on in obscure poverty at her sister's home until 1860, comforted to the end by the Bible, "my constant companion", given to her by Thomas Charles many years before. A society of Welsh-speaking nurses, the Beti Cadwaladr Society, proudly bears her name.

LADY LLANOVER
(1802–1896)

Lady Llanover was one of the most indefatigable champions of Welsh culture during the nineteenth century.

Born Augusta Waddington, the younger daughter of a Lincolnshire businessman who had settled in Monmouthshire, and the wife of Sir Benjamin Hall (later Baron Llanover and Abercarn, and the man after whom 'Big Ben' got its name), she became infatuated with all things Welsh and made it her mission to defend the cultural life of Wales by all possible means. Though never a fluent Welsh speaker herself she established her credentials at the Cardiff eisteddfod in 1834 with a prize-winning essay, in Welsh, 'On the Advantages resulting from the Preservation of the Welsh Language and the National Costume of Wales'.

Thereafter, proudly sporting her bardic name 'Gwenynen Gwent' ('the Bee of Gwent'), and ignoring the ridicule of the local gentry in this largely anglicised corner of Wales, she set out to make her home, Llanover Court, a centre of all things Welsh. She imported Welsh-speaking servants into her household. She dressed the women in bogus 'traditional' Welsh costumes (tall black hats, red shawls and petticoats), invented by Lady Llanover herself but which quickly became part of Welsh folklore. Supported by her husband who was himself a keen supporter of the Welsh language, she turned Llanover village into an oasis of Welshness, converting the Duke Inn into a temperance hotel (she was a fierce teetotaller) while the local Methodist chapel came to ring to rousing hymns sung by a Welsh-speaking congregation largely brought in from Cardiganshire, together with their pastor (beard

compulsory). In the early 1850s the Abercarn Colliery School was the only industrial school in south Wales to conduct its affairs through the medium of Welsh.

Though Lady Llanover certainly practised what she preached her influence extended well beyond the confines of her immediate community. She was, of course, a friend of Lady Charlotte Guest. Her obvious sincerity earned the respect of such distinguished patriots as the Rev. Thomas Price ('Carnhuanawc'), which led to her patronage of Cymreigyddion y Fenni, probably the most prominent Welsh society of the time, making Abergavenny one of the cultural hot-houses of Wales for some years. It was there, with her encouragement, that the important Welsh Manuscripts Society was formed and she acquired much of Iolo Morganwg's manuscript collection (now the Llanover Collection in the National Library of Wales). It was under her patronage that Ieuan Gwynedd's short-lived women's journal *Y Gymraes* was launched and she supported Daniel Silvan Evans in his mammoth project (and uncompleted: he got as far as 'E') to produce a Welsh equivalent to the Oxford English Dictionary. She was an ardent lover of harp music, facilitating the publication of collections of traditional Welsh airs and her resident harpist, the blind Thomas Gruffydd, was one of the foremost harpists of the time. In fact there was scarcely any aspect of Welsh life and culture which she failed to embrace with enthusiasm.

After her death she was laid to rest with her husband who had died thirty years previously, in an elaborate tomb in Llanover churchyard, escorted to her grave by twenty maidens dressed in traditional Welsh costume, her coffin bearing a wreath of white roses sent by the Duchess of Teck, later to become Queen Mary.

SIR HUGH OWEN
(1804–1881)

Nowhere is education valued more than in Wales. That is why Sir Hugh Owen's name is still honoured in his native land, for he was at the centre of all the important advances in education in Wales during the nineteenth century.

Born and bred in Anglesey he went to work in London where he became a clerk in the Poor Law Commission, rising to the position of Chief Clerk (more or less equivalent to a Permanent Secretary) in 1853. By then he had already established himself as a prominent voice in the advancement of education in Wales. Though always a committed Nonconformist he was no ideologue, his administrative mind seeking the most practical way of making progress. Therefore, in his famous *Letter to the Welsh People* issued in 1843, in the face of opposition from dogmatic Dissenters who sought progress through voluntary effort, Owen championed the use of state aid to advance non-denominational elementary education in Wales, in schools sponsored by the British and Foreign Schools Society. "Do not delay or the opportunity will be lost – lost for an age" he urged three years later, and the Welsh people heeded his call. Between 1843 and 1852 the number of British schools in north Wales rose from two to ninety and by 1870 there were over 300 British schools throughout Wales.

The expansion of British schools created a serious staffing shortage and it was largely thanks to Hugh Owen's drive that Bangor Normal College was established in 1858 as a teachers' training college for Wales, becoming in a few years a truly national institution ranking with the best of its kind in England. Owen employed the same zeal to the development of university education in Wales. Not only was he one of the leading figures in the formation of the University College of Wales at Aberystwyth in 1872 but, during the years of his retirement, he engaged in a personal crusade throughout Wales to raise money to keep the College in business. At the end of his life he was an influential adviser to the Aberdare Commission out of which were to emerge the first state secondary schools in the United Kingdom.

Professor Gwyn A Williams once described Hugh Owen as an "ambiguous hero", suggesting that, substantial though Owen's achievements were, his vision was limited. Rather than use the education system as a means of reinforcing the Welsh language and culture, his overriding mission was to create the conditions favourable to the emergence of a well-educated middle class in Wales able to make their way in the modern world with confidence. Certainly he never saw the need to teach Welsh to his own children. Nevertheless, a few months before his death, he was knighted for his services to Wales and, laid to rest in that Nonconformist Valhalla, Abney Park cemetery, he was surrounded by the leaders of all the main institutions of Wales, honouring what he had done for them.

RICHARD LEWIS
(Dic Penderyn) (1808/9–1831)

Richard Lewis, better known as 'Dic Penderyn', is generally revered as Wales' first working-class martyr.

Merthyr Tydfil, the crucible of the industrial revolution in south Wales, was the scene of a major working-class uprising in 1831, fuelled by political radicalism and economic depression, which resulted in fierce conflict between the local people and the forces of law and order. Several alleged ringleaders of the riots were brought before the Glamorgan Summer Assizes, including Richard Lewis, a young Penderyn labourer, who was accused of wounding a Scottish soldier outside the Castle Inn on 3 June, 1831.

It is now accepted that he was innocent of this specific offence. Nevertheless, in the face of conflicting evidence, he was regarded by the authorities as a ringleader of the mob and as the judge proclaimed: "I am inclined to think that an example in the person of an individual who actually commenced the attack may satisfy the exigency of public Justice."

A petition against his execution was signed by 11,000 people (almost the entire adult population of Merthyr Tydfil) and his cause was stoutly championed by the radical pacifist ironmaster, Joseph Tregelles Price of Neath. Convinced of his innocence after interviewing him in Cardiff gaol Price presented a formidably argued petition in person to the Home Secretary and the Lord Chancellor. He gained a stay of execution but for only a few days and Richard Lewis was publicly hanged in Cardiff on 13 August, uttering in Welsh the cry "O Lord, this is an injustice".

His body, accompanied by huge crowds, was taken to his birthplace, Aberavon, where it was first buried at the gate of St Mary's churchyard. Since then 'Dic Penderyn' has become transformed into a folk hero and his grave, now in the centre of the churchyard in the shadow of the M4 motorway and renovated by the Church in Wales, continues to be a place of pilgrimage for those interested in the history of the working-class movement.

HENRY RICHARD
(1812–1888)

Henry Richard was the greatest spokesman for Welsh Nonconformist radicalism in the mid-Victorian age.

Born in Tregaron, the son of one of the leading Presbyterian ministers of the day, he himself entered the ministry in 1835, serving as pastor to a Congregationalist chapel in London until 1848 when he became secretary of the London Peace Society. During the next few years, working with leading radicals like Richard Cobden and dubbed 'the Apostle of Peace' he strove tirelessly, at home and abroad, to get the principle of arbitration accepted as the only rational way of settling international disputes. He achieved success at the peace conference following the Crimean War when, for the first time in history, a clause was inserted in the Treaty of Paris, affirming the positive value of arbitration, not that this made much difference in years to come. Richard continued to campaign on this issue for the rest of his life, only relinquishing the secretaryship of the Peace Society in 1885, receiving a testimonial of four thousand guineas, a substantial sum in those days.

Richard's finest achievement was as the man who, more than any other, broke the mould of Welsh politics in the mid-Victorian era, heralding the triumph of Nonconformist radicalism over age-old feudalism. He first came into prominence as a spokesman for Welsh causes following the publication of the Reports of the Commissioners of Inquiry into the State of Education in Wales (*Y Llyfrau Gleision*). His critique of the reports, later published under the title *Letters on the Social and Political Condition of the Principality of Wales* was quite devastating and, robust Congregationalist that he was, he regarded the reports as a conspiracy by the Church of England to destroy Nonconformity in Wales.

Richard conducted his fightback via the Liberation Society, committed to the disestablishment of the Church of England. Although this was not a uniquely Welsh issue he made it into a national crusade. "Demand these things as a nation" he would cry, and the nation responded in the 1868 General Election, rounding on the Tory landed proprietors, the backbone of the Church of England, who had held sway for generations. "We are the Welsh nation, not you," proclaimed Richard. "This country is ours, and therefore we claim to have our principles and sentiments and feelings represented in the Commons." Seat after seat fell to the Liberals but the most remarkable result of all belonged to Henry Richard himself in Merthyr Tydfil where a newly enfranchised working class allied with radical Nonconformity swept him to victory. The Tory landlords of rural Wales fought back, evicting large numbers of tenants for having had the temerity to vote Liberal. Richard's passionate protests in the Commons contributed powerfully to the introduction of the secret ballot in 1872.

By now he was widely known as 'the Member for Wales'. He continued to involve himself in religious, land and education issues and commanded great respect up to his death. Sadly, though not surprisingly for someone who was as much at home in London as in Wales, he was buried in Abney Park cemetery, Stoke Newington, but a fine statue of him stands in the main square of the town of his birth.

DAVID DAVIES
(1818–1890)

Known to many of his contemporaries as 'Top Sawyer' because of his youthful prowess assisting his father in the Montgomeryshire sawmills, David Davies rose from rural obscurity to become the first Welsh industrial tycoon and was, in the opinion of his biographer Herbert Williams, "without doubt one of the most colourful characters ever to bestride the public stage of Wales".

There were three main phases in his phenomenal business career; first as the man who brought the railways to many parts of Wales, creating in the process the Talerddig cutting near Llanbrynmair, one of the wonders of Wales and at the time (1861) the deepest rock cutting in the world; secondly as the coal magnate whose company, the

Ocean Coal Co. Ltd., was at the time of his death the largest in south Wales; and thirdly as the man who, frustrated by the inertia of the Bute family, owners of the Cardiff docks, built Barry docks in the late 1880s as an outlet to the sea for his coal.

Despite his insistence that he was the Friend of the Working Man he became, much to his intense indignation, increasingly identified with other despotic south Wales industrialists like the Crawshays and the Vivians during a period of heightened class conflict in the 1870s and beyond. His early speeches in Parliament (he was Liberal MP for Cardiganshire from 1874 to 1886) attacked the drinking habits of the working man. He went so far as to propose that public houses in the countryside should be closed at 10 p.m. so that the labouring classes would be able to get up for work on time after a good night's sleep. He was also a strict sabbatarian, attending chapel three times on Sunday throughout his life, ideally back home in Llandinam, and refusing to transact any business and even to open letters on the Lord's Day. Davies is also remembered as the greatest benefactor of the University College of Wales, Aberystwyth, established in 1872.

His tendency to refer to himself with obvious approval as a self-made man could be irritating. Disraeli once observed dryly, "I am glad to hear the honourable member praising his creator".

The epitaph on his memorial in the north-east of Llandinam churchyard sums up his philosophy on life succinctly:

> Whatsoever thy hand findeth to do,
> do it with all thy might.
>
> (Ecclesiastes 9.10).

EVAN JONES
(Ieuan Gwynedd) (1820–1852)

One of the major milestones in the development of Welsh national consciousness during the nineteenth century was the appearance of, and the outcry against, the *Llyfrau Gleision*, the Blue Books containing the report of the educational commissioners sent to Wales to examine the state of education there (1847). While the commissioners' conclusion, that the state of education was dismal, was accurate enough the reasons given caused great offence. The three commissioners knew nothing about education and even less about Wales and their report constituted an ignorant and prejudiced attack on Welsh Nonconformity, and the Welsh language itself was described as "a manifold barrier to the moral progress".

Evan Jones (born near Dolgellau and popularly known as Ieuan Gwynedd) became acknowledged nationwide as one of the leading critics of the report. Having retired at the age of only twenty-seven from the Congregationalist ministry in Tredegar through ill-health he became one of the most gifted journalists of his day. In newspaper articles and pamphlets he subjected the report to scathing yet well-argued attack; what would people have said, he asked, if three monoglot Welshmen had been commissioned to examine the state of education in the counties of Norfolk, Bedfordshire and Staffordshire?

The commissioners had also issued a warning. As one of them wrote: "There is another very painful feature in the laxity of morals. I refer to the alleged want of chastity in the women. If this be so it is sufficient to account for all other immoralities, for each generation will derive its moral tone in a great degree from the influences imparted by the mothers who reared them." Ieuan Gwynedd took issue with this. In his *Facts, Figures and Statements in illustration of the Dissent and Morality of Wales: an Appeal to the English People* (1849) he produced statistics to show that in terms of illegitimate births Welsh women were no more profligate than English women. However Ieuan did not leave it at that. Under the patronage of the redoubtable Lady Llanover he became editor of the first Welsh publication aimed at the women of Wales, *Y Gymraes* (The Welshwoman). Its objective, during the two years of its existence, was to create "faithful girls, virtuous women, thrifty wives and intelligent mothers".

Sadly, Ieuan Gwynedd did not live to see the success of his campaign. He died at the early age of thirty-two and was buried in the cemetery of the historic Groeswen chapel, near Caerphilly. The cemetery came to be known as the 'Westminster Abbey of Wales' because of the large number of prominent Nonconformist ministers resting there, including the great William Williams ('Caledfryn'), described at the time of his death in 1869 as "a household word among the Welsh nation", and Tawelfryn Thomas, Ieuan Gwynedd's biographer.

MICHAEL DANIEL JONES
(1822–1898)

Without Michael D Jones there would surely never have been 'Y Wladfa' in Patagonia.

He succeeded his father, also named Michael Jones, as the principal of Bala Independent College, a seminary where Independent ministers were trained. Both father and son were combative and controversial men, frequently at odds with their co-religionists over matters of doctrine and organisation, but Michael D Jones went further.

Some have regarded him as the greatest Welshman of the nineteenth century. While there may be room for more than one view on this, what is certainly not in doubt was his bitter hostility against all things English, particularly the Tory landowners who, he believed, treated the common people of Wales (including his widowed mother who was evicted from her home by the Williams-Wynns) like serfs. He saw little value in escaping English oppression by going to the United States; he had personally witnessed how Welsh culture was diluted among the Welsh immigrants to Cincinnati.

As far as he was concerned the only real solution was to set up a brand new colony in virgin territory, miles from anywhere. Having read about Patagonia and heard the optimistic assessment of those he had sent out to assess the possibilities he persuaded the Argentine government to set aside land in the Chubut valley for a Welsh settlement, Nonconformist in religion and purely Welsh in language. In 1865 the *Mimosa* left Liverpool for Patagonia carrying 153 would-be settlers. The early years were hard – there were three ministers but only two farmers on board ship – but the settlers eventually succeeded in creating a colony which was to retain its essential Welshness up to the Second World War, and still survives to this day.

Michael D Jones, 'the vicarious Moses' (in Jan Morris' words) did not go to Patagonia himself though he sank, and lost, a good deal of his own money in the venture. Moreover, his son, Llwyd ap Iwan, who did go out, had the misfortune to be killed by some bandits in 1909 (but not, as is sometimes believed, by Butch Cassidy and the Sundance Kid, who were already dead by then). Jones himself remained in Wales where he was to educate a new generation of Welshmen, such as Thomas Ellis, David Lloyd George and Owen M Edwards, on the merits of Welsh nationalism.

Jones and his father lie side by side in the small cemetery, near to the door of the historic, but now closed, Hen Gapel, just outside Llanuwchllyn.

SIR JOHN WILLIAMS
(1840–1926)

Sir John Williams, royal physician, was one of Wales' greatest
benefactors. From humble beginnings in remotest Carmarthenshire
John Williams rose to become one of the most celebrated doctors of his
day. He was a favourite physician to the Royal Family and was made a
baronet in 1894. In 1896, on the death of his friend Sir William Jenner,
he acquired the lease to his house in London, where he lived until his
retirement in 1903.

During his professional life Sir John had built up a large collection
of rare books and manuscripts and on his retirement to Llansteffan he
immersed himself in the movement to establish a National Library for
Wales. Although some wanted the library located in Cardiff his voice in
favour of Aberystwyth was decisive. As far as he was concerned it was far
better to locate the library in a small quiet town – where the
accommodation was cheap – than in a place like Cardiff, full of hustle
and bustle and with a high cost of living. Moreover, he would deposit
his magnificent collection of books and manuscripts nowhere else but
Aberystwyth. And what a superb collection it was. The Peniarth
collection, originally collected by Robert Vaughan of Hengwrt in the
seventeenth century, included such priceless medieval manuscripts as
The White Book of Rhydderch which contains the earliest complete text
of *The Mabinogion, The Black Book of Carmarthen*, the earliest existing
manuscript in the Welsh language, *The Black Book of Chirk, The Book of
Taliesin* and Geoffrey of Monmouth's *History of the Kings of Britain.* He
also transferred to the library the book collection of Moses Williams,
the great eighteenth century antiquarian, who had managed to collect

most of the books published in Wales between 1546 and 1742.

Altogether, Sir John donated some 25,000 books and 1,200 manuscripts to the National Library of Wales. The material conveyed from his home in 116 chests weighed about twelve tons. When the National Library was officially opened by King George V and Queen Mary in 1911, the GCVO was conferred on its first President, none other than Sir John Williams.

Other notable achievements of this proud Welshman included his involvement in the establishment of a Welsh Hospital Unit sent out to South Africa during the Boer War, and the setting up of the widely acclaimed King Edward VII Welsh Memorial Association for the Prevention of Tuberculosis. He was also instrumental in having Wales identified separately from 'England and Wales' in the Medical Directory. After his death he was buried in Aberystwyth cemetery.

Writing of Sir John's "unique record of enlightened generosity and benefaction" Dr Emyr Wyn Jones, the distinguished medical historian, concluded: "The Welsh nation will always remember him with deep affection and will remain for ever in his debt."

JOSEPH PARRY
(1841–1903)

Joseph Parry was Wales' most popular composer. Born in Merthyr Tydfil, much of his early life was spent in Pennsylvania where the family had emigrated in 1853. Unlike his brother Henry, Joseph succeeded in avoiding the call-up into the Union army during the American Civil War, by paying others to take his place. Returning to Wales in the 1860s he quickly built up a considerable reputation as a composer and adjudicator at eisteddfodau and from 1873 to 1880 was the first professor of music at the University College of Wales, Aberystwyth. After establishing and running the Music College of Wales in Swansea for seven years he joined the University College of South Wales and Monmouthshire, Cardiff, in 1888 as Lecturer and Head of the Department of Music. He held this position for the rest of his life, having failed to be appointed Principal of the Guildhall School of Music in 1896, much to his disappointment.

Parry's work was immensely popular not only in Wales but among the Welsh communities in North America. A prolific composer, his best-remembered works include *Blodwen*, the first Welsh opera, the greatly loved, if banal, 'Myfanwy', written in the 1870s, and many hymn tunes including 'Sirioldeb', 'Côr Caersalem' and 'Aberystwyth' which, in the words of the *Western Mail* at the time of Parry's death, would be sung "as long as there is a Welshman left to sing them". The Welsh-language periodical *Y Geninen* felt able to describe Joseph Parry as "without doubt the most well-known Welshman in the world at the beginning of the twentieth century".

Parry's birthplace, Chapel Row in Merthyr Tydfil, is now preserved as a museum of his life and work. Aspects of his life were depicted by Jack Jones, another son of Merthyr, in his novel *Off to Philadelphia in the Morning* (1947). Parry's grave is marked by a striking white marble memorial with musical motifs, in the north-east section of St Augustine's churchyard, Penarth. Not far from this lifelong teetotaler lies Samuel Arthur Brain, the founder of Cardiff's best-known brewery!

SIR OWEN MORGAN EDWARDS
(1858–1920)

In presenting Sir Owen M Edwards to the University of Wales for
an honorary doctorate Sir John Morris-Jones proclaimed: "There is
no-one alive today who has done so much to prolong the life of the
Welsh language."

Born the eldest of four children at Llanuwchllyn, Merionethshire,
and a pupil at Bala grammar school, Owen was a brilliant scholar at
Balliol College, Oxford, where he helped to found the influential Welsh
literary society Cymdeithas Dafydd ap Gwilym. From 1889 to 1907 he
was Fellow and Tutor in History at Lincoln College.

He was, however, no elitist for his main mission in life was to instil
in the ordinary people of Wales ('*y werin*') a sense of pride in their
history, language and culture. To this end O M Edwards wrote several
books, in English and in Welsh, on the history and traditions of his
native country, including the elegant if rather unbalanced *Wales* (1901)
in the *Stories of the Nations* series (only about an eighth of the book
covered the period after the Act of Union!). His greatest literary
contribution was as the founder and editor of some of the most
influential periodicals ever produced in Wales, notably *Cymru*, a
monthly magazine launched in 1891, and for children *Cymru'r Plant*,
launched in the following year and which, in its heyday, sold 12,000
copies a month, reflecting the editor's skill in writing straightforward
Welsh, accessible to all.

In 1907 O M Edwards returned to live in Llanuwchllyn on his
appointment as the first Chief Inspector of Schools in Wales, and,
doing much of his paperwork at one end of the dining room table, he

was able to break down much of the stuffy formality of the past and, in particular, to improve the standing of Welsh in schools. The regulations governing the conduct of elementary and secondary education were immediately revised to encourage teaching in schools through the medium of Welsh in areas where Welsh was the mother tongue, and O M Edwards strove to ensure that the teachers' training colleges of Wales were able to produce an adequate supply of bilingual teachers.

For someone who cared as passionately as he did for Wales and who was such an inspiration to others, Edwards was anything but a political activist. He reluctantly became Liberal MP for Merioneth for a few months after Thomas Ellis' death but stood down at the 1900 General Election.

O M Edwards was knighted in 1916 and received his honorary doctorate from the University of Wales two years later. At the entrance to the village of Llanuwchllyn are bronze statues of Sir Owen and his son Sir Ifan, created in 1958 by the sculptor Jonah Jones. Sir Owen's grave is located in Capel y Pandy cemetery, in the centre of the village, entered through an elegant gateway erected to his memory.

THOMAS EDWARD ELLIS
(1859–1899)

Tom Ellis, the most prominent spokesman for the cause of Wales at the close of the nineteenth century, and regarded by some as the 'Parnell of Wales', was born in Cefnddwysarn, near Bala, the third of eight children of a tenant farmer. He attended Bala grammar school where he formed a close friendship with the young Owen M Edwards which was to last for the rest of his life.

His student years in Aberystwyth and Oxford fuelled his interest in politics and, inspired by the great Michael D Jones, was elected as Liberal MP for Merionethshire in 1886 as a passionate advocate of Home Rule for Wales so that, in the words of his election manifesto, "the control of the liquor trade, taxation, public appointments and the means of national development may be in the hands of the Welsh". For a few years he was a leading figure in the *Cymru Fydd* (the Wales of the Future) movement, a pressure group of the Welsh Liberal elite seeking to advance the cause of Wales politically and culturally.

Though Welsh Home Rule was undoubtedly a pipedream at the time, he was accused by some then and is still accused by some now of betraying and setting back the cause of Welsh Nationalism by accepting high office, as Junior Government Whip in 1892 and as Liberal Chief Whip in 1894, appointments which made quite sure that he could not 'rock the Liberal boat' during the 1890s. In fact, widely admired for his integrity and conscientiousness, he was probably too nice a person to manage the rough and tumble of Liberal politics in the post-Gladstonian era. Certainly Asquith felt that he was "more at home among the children of light than with the children of this world, with whom a Chief Whip is in daily and even hourly converse", and R B Haldane thought that Ellis' premature death in 1899 was probably timely in terms of his historical reputation.

Nevertheless, he was widely mourned as an elegant and committed advocate of the cause of Wales and his achievement is commemorated by a statue standing prominently in Bala High Street. He once edited some of the works of the great Puritan writer Morgan Llwyd, whose words are quoted on the memorial: "A man's time is his inheritance and woe to him who wastes it." (trans.). A substantial Celtic cross marks Ellis' grave in Cefnddwysarn cemetery.

DAVID LLOYD GEORGE
(1863–1945)

David Lloyd George, Prime Minister during the First World War, was the first outsider to get to the top of the 'greasy pole' of British politics.

Winston Churchill considered Lloyd George (who was actually born and spent the first two years of his life in Manchester) as "the greatest Welshman that unconquerable race has produced since the age of the Tudors". Regarded by many as a devious and unprincipled operator, his career was characterised by inconsistency, or by what some would call pragmatism, and his main driving force was a determination to get things done. As Chancellor of the Exchequer in Asquith's Liberal Government he laid the foundations of the welfare state; as Prime Minister he, more than anyone else, was the architect of victory in the First World War and achieved a settlement of sorts to the Irish Question.

After his fall from power in 1922 he never again held government office. Retiring from the House of Commons in 1945 after representing Caernarfon Boroughs for over fifty years he was briefly elevated to the House of Lords as Earl Lloyd George of Dwyfor and Viscount Gwynedd, thereby joining an institution he had denounced in 1909 as "a body of five hundred men chosen at random from among the unemployed".

A keen *Cymru Fydd* home ruler during his political youth Lloyd George appeared to lose interest in the issue as he climbed the political ladder. However, it is interesting to note that during the second trial, in London, of Saunders Lewis and the other Penyberth aerodrome arsonists in 1936, in a private letter to his daughter he wrote with some emotion: "This is the first government that has tried to put Wales on trial in the Old Bailey. I should like to be there, and I should like to be forty years younger."

His friend D R Daniel observed a lack of consistency in Lloyd George's makeup in other respects too. His unpublished memoir of Lloyd George in the National Library of Wales provides an excellent insight into his character and personality. He writes, for instance, that while Lloyd George had great respect for the Nonconformist conscience in others, "there was never since the days of Charles the Second's roisterers a man with less of it himself".

Whatever his shortcomings, his achievement, as an ordinary Welshman with no advantages of birth, in storming the citadels of the Establishment to become a world statesman, while always retaining his national identity gave, and still gives, Welsh people everywhere a genuine sense of pride. His grave, by the edge of the river Dwyfor in the village of Llanystumdwy and designed by his friend Clough Williams-Ellis, must be in one of the most beautiful locations anywhere.

ARTHUR GOULD
(1864–1919)

Arthur 'Monkey' Gould is generally acknowledged as the finest of all Welsh rugby players, "the W G Grace of Welsh rugby" in the words of that most authoritative of rugby writers, JBG Thomas.

Gould had acquired the nickname 'monkey' during his youth because of his ability to climb trees, and certainly not because of his appearance. Indeed, during his heyday in the 1890s, his handsome face appeared everywhere, even on the cover of match boxes, such was his standing as Welsh Rugby Union's first superstar.

He played first class rugby from 1882 to 1898, mainly at centre three-quarter. Although some of his career took place in England, his profession as a public works contractor taking him far and wide, the beginning and end were spent at Newport for whom he scored 554 points, including 136 tries (39 of them in 1892/3 alone). He played for Wales on 27 occasions, 18 times as captain; he led Wales when they won the Triple Crown for the first time in 1893.

The end of his international career was surrounded by controversy. He was accused of professionalism for benefiting from the proceeds of a testimonial, launched after his final, victorious appearance against England in 1897. The fund raised the considerable sum of £400, enough to buy the house in Newport where he was to live for the rest of his life, the title deeds being presented to him by none other than the President of the Welsh Rugby Union. For a time the ensuing row threatened to cause a permanent rift between Wales and the other three home countries, until Gould issued a statement undertaking never to play again for Wales, an empty pledge as he had already retired from the game.

This did not prevent him from serving as a referee, as a member of the Welsh Rugby Union Executive and as a national selector for several years. He also took up cricket and golf and was a sidesman at the church of St John the Baptist, Risca Road, Newport, where his large funeral took place in January 1919, following 'the immortal' Arthur Gould's unexpected death. He was buried in St Woolo's cemetery. The *Daily Express* paid him a handsome tribute: "Sure-footed, fast and the lucky owner of a bewildering swerve, he was a giant among giants."

After his death an Arthur Gould Memorial Bed was endowed at the Royal Gwent Hospital in his memory. Above the bed was a brass plaque which read: "To the memory of Arthur Gould, the greatest of all rugby football players…this bed is dedicated by admirers in five continents."

BILLY MEREDITH
(1874–1958)

Billy Meredith was soccer's first superstar. Born at Chirk, the son of a coal miner, Billy himself worked down the local pit for some years until, after several successful seasons in Welsh League football, he signed as a professional with Manchester City in 1894. Playing on the right wing he was the dominant force in the side for a decade, primarily responsible for the team's promotion to the First Division, and by scoring the winning goal in the 1904 Cup Final Billy became the first Welshman to captain a cup-winning team. By then he was the most popular footballer in the country, as much a household name as politicians and music hall entertainers. He was invariably depicted by newspaper cartoonists of his day chewing on a toothpick, a lifelong habit of his.

Billy's suspension for several months for attempting to bribe the Aston Villa captain into 'throwing' a crucial championship match in April 1905 ("had I been anyone but a Welshman I would have been better dealt with") did remarkably little to diminish his standing in the game. He joined Manchester United in 1906 and although by now a relative veteran, Billy was a major force in a team that won the League championship in 1908 and 1911, and the FA Cup in 1909. He continued playing during the war years and spent the last three years of his long career back at Manchester City, making his final appearance at a Cup semi-final match in 1924 at the remarkable age of forty-nine.

His international career lasted almost as long. He occasionally mused that had he been born a few hundred yards to the east he would have qualified to play for England. Nevertheless, he proudly pulled on the Welsh jersey in 48 official internationals between 1895 and 1920, his most memorable game being his last when Wales beat England 2-1 away, to win the Home Championship for only the second time.

Billy Meredith's dominance of the game for so long was based on his peerless ball control, his passing skills and his outstanding ability to score goals, particularly during his early career with Manchester City (in 1898/99 he scored 29 goals in 33 League games, an unheard of performance for a winger). After his retirement he continued to enjoy celebrity status, appearing as himself in a popular silent movie, *The Ball of Fortune,* in 1926 and giving anyone who asked, whether in the public house he ran in Manchester, in the press or as an after-dinner speaker, his views about the modern game and the good old days.

In 1996 Billy Meredith, the 'Welsh Wizard', was one of six players shortlisted for inclusion in a series of postage stamps commemorating all-time football legends.

STEPHEN OWEN DAVIES
(1886–1972)

To call S O Davies a politician is to diminish his impact as "one of the most colourful, controversial and independent of the MPs elected from the Welsh mining valleys", the words used by the *Western Mail* at the time of his death. The *South Wales Echo* described him as a "pacifist, a Socialist and a patriotic Welshman".

Born in the Cynon Valley in 1886 (or it might have been 1883) he was, as a young man, excluded from the Brecon Memorial College (a Congregationalist foundation) for his radical religious beliefs and, after serving for some years as a combative miners' leader, S O Davies was elected Labour MP for Merthyr Tydfil in 1934, a seat he held until his death.

He was not, strictly speaking, a pacifist; he simply opposed what he regarded as capitalist or imperialist wars and this often appeared to give him an anti-West and pro-communist bias. He was certainly a socialist and this brought him into frequent conflict with successive Labour governments of the day. He went so far as to boycott the ceremony at which Harold Wilson, then Prime Minister, was given the Freedom of the Borough of Merthyr Tydfil because of what he regarded as the Government's cynical response to the Aberfan disaster. As a lifelong supporter of Welsh self-government, S O Davies remained a minority voice in his party and, to the sneers of many of his colleagues, he proudly acted as one of Gwynfor Evans' sponsors when he was introduced to the House of Commons after Plaid Cymru's historic win in the Carmarthen by-election in 1966.

Deselected by his local party, only partly on grounds of age,

S.O.Davies stood as an Independent Socialist in the 1970 General Election and won by a mile, the only politician within living memory to beat the party machine. He was promptly expelled from the Labour party. Characteristically, his last appearance in the House of Commons, a few days before he died, was to vote against the Common Market. After a rousing funeral, S O Davies was buried at Maes-yr-arian cemetery, Mountain Ash.

HEDD WYN
(Ellis Humphrey Evans) (1887–1917)

Despite the fact that Paul Turner's film *Hedd Wyn* was shortlisted for
an Oscar in the 'best foreign film' category in 1992 and received the
Royal Television Society Best Drama award, it is sad that the film has
failed to secure a distributor in England. This is a shame because the
story of Hedd Wyn's short but dramatic life deserves a wide audience.

'Hedd Wyn' was the bardic name of a shepherd, Ellis Humphrey
Evans, born and brought up in the Trawsfynydd area. He was a regular
and highly regarded competitor at the provincial eisteddfodau and was
runner-up in the Chair competition at the National Eisteddfod in
Aberystwyth (one of the three adjudicators ranked him first). In 1917
he submitted a poem, ironically entitled *'Yr Arwr'* ('The Hero') for the
Chair competition at the National Eisteddfod at Birkenhead, using the
bardic name 'Fleur de Lis' for a change. When the winner's name was
called out there was no response for, six weeks earlier, having enlisted
with the 15th Battalion of the Royal Welsh Fusiliers in the spring,
Hedd Wyn had been killed in the battle for Pilkem Ridge at Ypres.
As the *Western Mail* reported: "Instead of the usual chairing ceremony
the chair was draped in a black funeral pall amidst death-like silence,
and the bards came forward in long procession to place their muse-
tribute of englyn or couplet on the draped chair in memory of the dead
bard hero."

Hedd Wyn immediately achieved the status of a Welsh Rupert
Brooke and after the war, following a successful campaign, the
Commonwealth War Graves Commission agreed that his headstone
should read not 'E H Evans' but '*Y Prifardd Hedd Wyn*'. As the leader

of the campaign, Silyn Roberts, himself a distinguished poet, explained to the Commission: "Although a young man and a young peasant his name was a household word in Wales on account of the great distinction he had attained as a Poet. He was everywhere known in Wales as Hedd Wyn and comparatively few people outside his parish knew that his name was E H Evans. Consequently the inscription of his Bardic name on the head-stone would assist Welsh visitors to find his grave."

The celebrated poet R Williams Parry wrote a series of notable englynion in Hedd Wyn's memory. In the middle of Trawsfynydd stands a fine bronze statue of our hero, dressed in shepherd's clothing, unveiled by his mother in 1923. On the plaque is a verse composed by Hedd Wyn mourning the death of a friend from Ffestiniog killed in action:

> Ei aberth nid â heibio – a'i wyneb
> Annwyl nid â'n ango,
> Er i'r Almaen ystaenio
> Ei dwrn dur yn ei waed o.

(Neither his sacrifice nor his dear countenance are forgotten, though the Hun has stained his fist of steel in his blood.)

JAMES GRIFFITHS
(1890–1975)

James Griffiths, one of ten children born and brought up in the mining community of Betws, Ammanford, is now one of the forgotten heroes of Welsh public life in the twentieth century. After working in the mines in his youth he became an effective miners' agent, eventually becoming President of the Miners Federation of South Wales during the Depression years.

He represented Llanelli as a Labour MP from 1936 until 1970 and, with Aneurin Bevan, shares the credit for the establishment of the Welfare State in the post-war period, serving as Minister for National Insurance in Attlee's administration, followed by a year as Colonial Secretary. Though lacking Aneurin Bevan's charisma Griffiths, as Deputy Leader under Hugh Gaitskell, was highly regarded as a team player and did much to keep the Labour Party more or less united in opposition.

Though never a Welsh nationalist in the political sense he always retained a deep commitment to the maintenance of Welsh life and culture (he was a strong supporter of the National Eisteddfod movement) and became a gradual convert to political devolution for Wales. He was responsible for persuading Gaitskell to include the establishment of a Secretary of State for Wales in the 1959 Labour Party Manifesto, and it was fitting that when Labour came to power in 1964 Jim Griffiths was appointed the first Secretary of State for Wales, with a seat in the Cabinet. This was the crowning achievement of a life full of accomplishment and he served in the position from 1964 to 1966. Though he retired from the House of Commons in 1970 he remained an influential advocate of political devolution for Wales. Indeed it is said that he persuaded Harold Wilson not to appoint George Thomas as Secretary of State for Wales in 1974 because of the harm it would do to the Welsh cause.

After his death Jim Griffiths was buried in a simple grave in the near left-hand corner of the cemetery behind the Christian Temple, Ammanford, the chapel where he had grown up, a modest memorial for someone who did so much to shape modern Wales.

WILLIAM JAMES WILDE
(1892–1969)

Jimmy Wilde, one of Britain's greatest ever boxers, had at least four highly evocative nicknames, 'the Mighty Atom', 'the Tylorstown Terror', 'the Ghost with a Hammer in his Hand' and 'the Indian Famine' and in his prime he stood no more than 5 feet 3 inches tall and weighed less than seven stone.

A coal miner at the age of twelve, Jimmy started his fighting career in the boxing booths and fairgrounds of south Wales to supplement his meagre income, earning five shillings in his first bout and catching the eye of the local promoters. After winning the Welsh flyweight championship in 1912 he won the British and European titles two years later. Having lost the British title he was to regain it in 1916, going on to defeat, in the twelfth round of a twenty-round contest, the Italian American Young Zulu Kid for the World Championship on 18 December 1916 in London. He lost the crown in New York in 1923 when Pancho Villa knocked him out in the seventh round, though Villa should probably have been disqualified after the end of round two for delivering a foul blow after the bell had rung.

Wilde immediately retired from boxing after a career embracing 153 officially recorded fights (losing only four), almost one fight a month over a fourteen-year period, including five contests in the month of September 1913 alone. It is estimated that he fought 700 more in the boxing booths, invariably against opponents substantially heavier than himself. For some years he was doorman at the *News of the World* and lent his name to a weekly boxing column in the newspaper. He also wrote his autobiography, *Fighting was my Business,* in 1938.

His last years were rather sad. He never really recovered from being severely beaten up by a gang of teenage thugs at a lonely railway station on the way home from a charity function and, tenderly cared for by the nurses, Jimmy Wilde was to pass away in Whitchurch Hospital, Cardiff, unaware that his wife had already died four years before. He joined her in Merthyr Dyfan cemetery, Barry, where his headstone carries the simple epitaph: "Ex-flyweight champion of the world".

SAUNDERS LEWIS
(1893–1985)

In some respects the least typical of Welshmen, born and brought up in the Welsh bourgeois community of Liverpool, and a fervent convert to the Roman Catholic faith, John Saunders Lewis is widely regarded as one of the most influential Welshmen of the twentieth century.

As a writer and critic he was unsurpassed in the breadth and quality of his work and he enjoyed a high reputation well beyond the confines of the United Kingdom. His plays, ranging from themes deep in the history of Wales to contemporary issues, were evocative of European writers as diverse as Pierre Corneille and Jean-Paul Sartre and his erudite literary criticisms strove to place Welsh literature, notably the hymns of William Williams Pantycelyn, within a wider European context.

Influenced by patriotic writers like Emrys ap Iwan, Saunders Lewis became a passionate Welsh nationalist, again seeing Wales as part of the community of European nations. He was a founder member of the Welsh Nationalist party, Plaid Cymru, in 1925 and served as its president until 1939. Two events in his political career stand out. Together with D J Williams and the Rev. Lewis Valentine he took part in an arson attack on a bombing school at Penyberth on the Llŷn peninsula in 1936. They immediately gave themselves up to the police and at the subsequent trial at Caernarfon Saunders Lewis vigorously defended their action:

> We hold with unshakeable conviction that the burning of the
> monstrous bombing range in Llŷn was an act forced upon us for
> the defence of Welsh civilization, for the defence of Christian
> principles, for the maintenance of the Law of God in Wales.

Though the jury, all Welsh speakers, failed to convict, Lewis and his colleagues were retried at the Old Bailey, found guilty and sentenced to nine months' imprisonment. Lewis was also dismissed from his lecturing post at University College, Swansea.

Saunders Lewis believed that the future of Wales as a distinct community depended crucially on the continuing vitality of the Welsh language. In 1962 he gave the BBC Welsh Region's annual radio lecture on *Tynged yr Iaith* ('The fate of the Language') in which he stated that "Wales without the Welsh language will not be Wales", but warned that unless something was done "Welsh will end as a living language about the beginning of the twenty first century".
The broadcast immediately led to the formation of *Cymdeithas yr Iaith Gymraeg* ('The Welsh Language Society') of which Saunders Lewis became honorary president.

After his death he was buried in the Roman Catholic section of Penarth cemetery.

SIR IFAN ap OWEN EDWARDS
(1895–1970)

The distinguished son of a distinguished father, Ifan ap Owen Edwards was one of Wales' greatest twentieth century patriots. Inheriting his father's passionate love of his country, on Sir Owen's death in 1920 Ifan continued to edit, with great zeal, *Cymru* and *Cymru'r Plant*.

Indeed he quickly transformed *Cymru'r Plant* into a vehicle for launching, in 1922, what became his life's work, *Urdd Gobaith Cymru* ('the Welsh League of Youth'). According to the Urdd Manifesto of 1929 its aim was to:

> create an undefiled Welsh Wales, not for its own sake, not in any
> attempt to make Wales superior to other countries, but in order
> that Wales can play its part in bringing peace to a world which
> today is too ready to display a spirit of antagonism and war.

The Urdd organised summer camps and annual eisteddfodau attended by thousands of children and at the height of its influence in the mid-1930s it could boast a membership of 50,000, though in its ethos this children's crusade could not have been further removed from the nationalistic European youth movements of the decade. Though always the driving force of the Urdd, Ifan only became its president in 1944, a position he retained until his death.

Ifan was a pioneer in other respects too. Consistent with his determination to promote respect for Welsh life and culture, in 1935 Ifan produced *Y Chwarelwr* (The Quarryman), the first talking picture ever made in the Welsh language, a powerful documentary portraying the everyday lives of the quarrymen of Blaenau Ffestiniog and their families. In 1939, partly in order to create a totally Welsh-speaking environment in which his young son could be educated, he established in Aberystwyth the first primary school in Wales where pupils were taught through the medium of Welsh.

Like his father before him Ifan was knighted for his services to Wales (1947) and awarded an honorary doctorate by the University of Wales (1959). He also served for some years as a director of TWW, the Welsh commercial TV channel.

The striking modernist memorial over his grave in Llanuwchllyn cemetery was designed by his son Prys.

SIR CYNAN EVANS-JONES
(1895–1970)

There must have been something special about 'Cynan' (the bardic name of Albert Evans-Jones) for BBC Wales to have devoted its first ever colour film to his life and times, *Cynan, y llanc o Lŷn* ('Cynan', the lad from Llŷn). The fact is that by the late 1960s few names were better known, or faces more immediately recognised, than his.

A north Walian from Pwllheli, the town that made him a Freeman in 1963, Cynan, a shopkeeper's son, graduated from the University College of North Wales, Bangor, in 1916 and saw war service, first with the 86th Field Ambulance Corps, then as a chaplain, in Salonica and France. His experiences stimulated him to write some fine poetry; indeed he has been called the Siegfried Sassoon of Wales for his graphic and poignant verse. His Crown-winning *pryddest* (long, free-metre poem) at the National Eisteddfod of 1921, *'Mab y Bwthyn'* ('Son of the Cottage'), is considered by Dafydd Owen, a leading authority on the work of Cynan, as "the most widely read, memorised and quoted of all Welsh poems in the first half of the century".

During the 1920s Cynan served as a Presbyterian minister in Penmaenmawr, before taking up an appointment as extra-mural lecturer at his old College in 1931, specialising in Welsh literature and drama, until his retirement in 1960. No-one was better qualified to fill such a post. He was three times winner of the Crown and once of the Chair at the National Eisteddfod, and was acknowledged as an authority on Welsh drama. His own play about Howel Harris won the drama prize at the Bangor Eisteddfod of 1931, the same year as he was awarded the Crown for his poem *'Y Dyrfa'* ('The Crowd'). Also in 1931, such was his standing, he was appointed by the Lord Chamberlain as the first censor of Welsh plays, a position he retained until its abolition in 1968.

However, Cynan's finest contribution to the life of Wales was as the embodiment of its greatest manifestation of Welsh identity, the National Eisteddfod. He was the only person to be elected Archdruid twice (1950–1953 and 1963–1967) and, reflecting his own theatrical bent, he was, more than anyone else, responsible for the colourful spectacle which characterises the modern national eisteddfod, including the introduction of the Flower Dance. Indeed Cynan once described the Gorsedd of Bards as the "National Pageant of Wales" and worked hard to ensure that it became "a truly dignified symbol of the spirit of a nation".

Awarded the CBE in 1947, and an honorary Doctorate from the University of Wales in 1961, he was knighted in 1969 for services to the cultural life of Wales, at which point Albert Evans-Jones incorporated his bardic name into his own, being thereafter known as Sir Cynan Evans-Jones. Following his death he was buried in that most evocative of resting places, Church Island, near Menai Bridge.

ANEURIN BEVAN
(1897–1960)

Aneurin Bevan, born in Tredegar the son of a miner, had no doubt about his credentials. "I am a Welshman, a Socialist representing a Welsh constituency," he proclaimed during a parliamentary debate on the National Health Service in 1948. Admittedly, despite the fact that his father was a Welsh speaker Aneurin never showed much interest in the Welsh language or its culture, nor did he ever regard Wales as a distinct entity in political terms. Nevertheless, his greatest achievements were rooted in his Welsh environment. He was, to coin Dai Smith's phrase, "indissolubly knitted into the Welsh fabric". Bevan loved the music of the south Wales valleys and he was one of the very few national figures to show any appreciation of the work of that great Welsh poet, Idris Davies, during his lifetime.

It was in the Nonconformist south Wales valleys that Bevan, never a chapel goer himself, developed a speaking style that made him perhaps the finest orator of his time. And his oratory was never empty rhetoric; each speech "due to Welsh influence was a sermon" according to his great friend and agent Archie Lush. For Bevan, a Marxist firebrand steeped in the labour struggles of south Wales in the 1920s, was a crusader. Entering Parliament in 1929 as MP for Ebbw Vale he was determined to expose unflinchingly to the London establishment the brutal hardships experienced by the communities from which he sprang. "I never used to regard myself so much as a politician as a projectile discharged from the Welsh valleys," he once admitted and when, in 1948, he famously denounced the Tories as "lower than vermin", bringing down unprecedented wrath on his head, he was unrepentant.

"When I listen to the cacophony of harsh voices trying to intimidate I close my eyes and listen to the silent voices of the poor."

When he was appointed Minister of Health in the 1945 Labour Government Bevan seized the chance to establish a free national health service with both hands. Some of the ground had been prepared in the Beveridge Report. However, Bevan, recalling the hardships of inter-war south Wales and inspired by the egalitarian principles on which the Tredegar Working Men's Medical Aid Society had been based, had a personal mission to achieve. Applying socialist zeal and Welsh determination, Bevan effectively nationalised British medicine, bringing about the most far-reaching piece of social legislation in the country's history.

Throughout his career Aneurin had his critics. Churchill once called him a "squalid nuisance". Some called him a "Champagne socialist", hardly a serious charge. Others, with more substance, accused him of being a poor team player who, had he played the political game differently, could have become Labour leader. Who knows? What is certain is that when he died the whole country united in grief, but most of all the ordinary people of south Wales whose constant champion he had been. John Morgan put it well: "The sadness was of a kind which would probably seem peculiar in parts of the country where heroes seldom embody with such extraordinary fidelity the attitudes and history, the exacting character and dreams of place and people."

DAVID JAMES JONES
('Gwenallt') (1899–1968)

The sad thing about David James Jones, generally known by his bardic name 'Gwenallt', is that, despite being widely regarded as the greatest poet of the twentieth century in the Welsh language, he is so little known or appreciated outside his native land. However, drawing on his own rich and varied life, as an illuminator and interpreter of the broad and often seemingly contradictory aspects of Welsh life and culture, he stands supreme.

Born in Pontardawe and brought up in nearby Alltwen, he started and ended his life as a strongly committed Calvinistic Methodist, though fiercely embracing atheistic Marxism on the journey; during the First World War he was imprisoned as a conscientious objector, refusing to fight a capitalist war, later writing a novel based on his painful experiences, *Plasau'r Brenin* (The King's Mansions). He was a popular academic at University College of Wales, Aberystwyth, for thirty-nine years and won the Chair at the National Eisteddfod twice. He became the first editor of the influential literary journal *Taliesin.* He was a strong supporter of the Welsh nationalist cause.

Ned Thomas has written that Gwenallt "is our national poet of the century not because he celebrates Wales but because he expresses passions and tensions at work here without leaving anything out". He had the unique ability to express in elegant, evocative, sometimes angry, often poignant verse some of the recurring themes of Welsh life during the twentieth century. One such theme was Christianity and the challenge of Socialism, when, drawing very much on his own experience, he saw no fundamental conflict between the two, uttering the famous line: "There is a place for the fist of Karl Marx in His Church." Another theme was that of industrial deprivation and threats to the stability of Welsh rural life by alien and insensitive forces:

> We have exchanged our countrymen, our farms and our smallholdings
> For the industrial Mammon and the cheap bread.

In one of his best-loved works, '*Rhydcymerau*' (where his friend D J Williams lived), Gwenallt deplored the assault on the hillsides of his beloved Carmarthenshire, with conifers destroying a rich Welsh heritage:

> Trees where once was a community,
> A forest where once were farms.

Gwenallt has also been described as Wales' greatest Christian poet since William Williams, Pantycelyn. Certainly no Welsh poet has been more often quoted from the pulpit in the last fifty years and it is fitting that the words of William Williams were on Gwenallt's lips when he died in December 1968. He now lies in Aberystwyth cemetery under a striking slab of Welsh slate, a few yards from his university teacher, the great T Gwynn Jones.

WILFRED WOOLLER
(1912–1997)

In the records of Thornhill cemetery, Cardiff, Wilfred Wooller is described as a "retired journalist", but in his time he had been rather more than that. Indeed, he is remembered as one of Wales' twentieth century sporting giants.

Born and brought up in Colwyn Bay, Wilfred Wooller was an outstanding all-round sportsman. He represented Wales at squash and was good enough to play, briefly, centre forward for Cardiff City. However, rugby and cricket were the two sports at which he truly excelled, becoming a Cambridge Blue in both.

He made his debut for the Wales XV in 1933, the first occasion when Wales beat England at Twickenham. Altogether he played eighteen times at centre for Wales between 1933 and 1939, including the memorable victory against the All Blacks in 1935, and captained the team in 1939.

The Second World War, much of which he spent as a Japanese POW in the Far East, finished his rugby career but not his county cricket career which had begun in 1938. An effective all-rounder he was appointed captain of Glamorgan in 1947 and in the following year led the team to its first County Championship. He was, more than once, close to selection to the English team (some even regarding him as a possible captain). He actually turned down the chance to be vice-captain of the MCC touring team to South Africa in 1948/49 for business reasons. He was still able to achieve the double of one thousand runs and one hundred wickets in a season at the age of forty-one and continued to play for Glamorgan until he was nearly fifty.

Wilfred Wooller acted as a highly respected Test selector from 1955 to 1962 during a golden era of English cricket and after his retirement from the game he served as Secretary and later President of Glamorgan, combining his administrative responsibilities with journalism (*The Sunday Telegraph*) and media work. His live television commentary when Garfield Sobers, playing for Nottinghamshire, struck Malcolm Nash for six sixes in one over at Swansea in 1968, remains one of the great moments of British sports broadcasting.

A man of strong right-wing opinions, he was never afraid to express controversial views, notably in favour of maintaining sporting links with South Africa during the 1970s and 1980s. "These anti's make me puke", he once famously wrote in the *Western Mail*.

Speaking at the official opening of the Wilfred Wooller memorial gates at Sophia Gardens, Cardiff, in June 2001 the legendary Tom Graveney said of Wooller: "He was a great man and one of the great sporting heroes of Wales."

GWYNFOR EVANS
(born 1912)

Gwynfor Evans, after a lifetime of achievement, is now Wales' 'elder statesman'. Though born and brought up in Barry Gwynfor Evans' roots were in Carmarthenshire. After studying Law at Aberystwyth and Oxford he settled in Llangadog at the beginning of the Second World War, earning a living as a market gardener while promoting the causes of Plaid Cymru and pacifism to which he had become firmly committed during his student days.

In 1945 he was elected President of Plaid Cymru, a position he continued to hold until 1981, making him the longest-serving leader of a British political party in modern times. In 1949 he became a member of Carmarthenshire County Council, and during the next twenty-five years won several worthwhile victories in the battle to assert Welsh identity within the county.

On a wider stage Gwynfor Evans' skilful leadership of the campaign to save Cwm Tryweryn from drowning in the late 1950s and early 1960s brought him into the forefront of national politics. Although the campaign failed in its immediate objective it united Welsh opinion in an unprecedented fashion and persuaded many for the first time that self-government for Wales was the only remedy in the face of what appeared to be British intransigence.

However, Gwynfor Evans, a leading member of the Welsh Congregationalists and a thoroughly decent and cultured man (whose historical writings have done much to educate Welsh people about their rich heritage), attracted respect from a much wider community than those primarily striving for Welsh independence. It was fitting that,

after several attempts, he should become Plaid Cymru's first ever MP, winning Carmarthen in a historic by-election on 14 July 1966 (a result that even made the front page of *Pravda*). Though he lost the seat in 1970 he regained Carmarthen in October 1974 and during the next few years, leading a group of three Plaid Cymru MPs, he was able to secure important concessions for Wales from an embattled Labour Government.

Nevertheless, at the 1979 General Election, Gwynfor Evans again lost his seat and the incoming Conservative Government, encouraged by Wales' decisive rejection of an Assembly in the recent referendum, decided to renege on their policy to establish a Welsh-language TV channel. On 5 May 1980 Gwynfor announced his firm intention to fast unto death unless the Government changed its mind. Left in no doubt as to the resolve of this principled patriot the Government backed down. The graffiti on the Thames Embankment read 'Gwynfor 1 Thatcher 0'; characteristically Lady Thatcher made no reference to this defeat in her subsequent memoirs.

In August 2000, at the Llanelli National Eisteddfod, Gwynfor Evans, at the age of eighty-eight, was honoured as the first recipient of the newly-created annual World-Wide Welsh Award, a fitting tribute to one of the greatest Welshmen of the twentieth century.

THOMAS FARR
(1913–1986)

Born in Tonypandy, Tommy Farr, widely regarded as the greatest of all British-born heavyweight boxers, went into the sport to escape the mines, and by the age of twenty-one had won the Welsh light-heavyweight and heavyweight championships. In 1937 he defeated Ben Foord to become British and Empire heavyweight champion, and wins over Max Baer and Walter Neusel entitled him to challenge the great Joe Louis for the World crown. The fight took place at New York's Yankee Stadium on 30 August 1937 and was broadcast in the middle of the night to thousands of listeners back in Britain, huddled round their wireless sets or standing in the streets of the south Wales valleys listening to loudspeakers. Although Farr fought gamely and went the distance, objective observers judged Louis to be the clear winner, and Farr himself later joked, "the very mention of Louis' name still makes my nose bleed". Nevertheless his courageous performance made him a star. He relinquished his British title to cash in on his newly-found celebrity status in the United States (his Empire title was taken from him), but after a string of defeats he returned to Britain where he retired from the ring at the outbreak of the war.

Ironically rejected for army service as medically unfit, Tommy Farr pursued a number of unsuccessful business ventures during and after the war before making a boxing comeback in 1951. After some success, including regaining the Welsh heavyweight championship, he gave up for good in 1953 after losing to Don Cockel.

For twenty years he wrote a weekly boxing column for the *Sunday Pictorial* and afterwards acted as a representative for a paint firm. He also had a good singing voice and during his heyday recorded some pleasant ballads including 'Remember Me' when he was accompanied by George Formby on his ukelele.

After his death on St David's Day, 1986, Tommy Farr was cremated in Worthing. His ashes were brought back to the Rhondda for an emotional Welsh funeral full of choirs and rousing hymns, following which they were placed in an elegant grave he had erected for his parents in Trealaw cemetery. His epitaph reads:

> I claim that man
> Is master of himself
> When he can stand life's blows and scars
> And leave this world a better place behind him.

The manuscript of his autobiography was found among his papers after his death and was published in 1989 with the title *Thus Farr*.

RONALD STUART THOMAS
(1913–2000)

R S Thomas was a controversial figure. It is hardly surprising that when he died some of the broadsheets could not resist illustrating their obituary notices with Howard Barlow's well-known photograph of the old man glowering out of the open window of his retirement home on the Llŷn peninsula, as if this encapsulated the essence of the person.

To some extent it did. "Happiness", he once said, "I don't understand about happiness", and much of his poetry and other writings revealed an unusually depressing outlook on life for a man of the Anglican cloth whose main mission was to convey messages of hope. However, constantly beset by religious self-doubt, he would write ('In Church'):

> There is no other sound
> In the darkness but the sound of a man
> Breathing, testing his faith
> On emptiness, nailing his questions
> One by one to an untenanted cross.

He had a poor opinion of his compatriots, described in one of his most evocative poems, 'Welsh Landscape', as:

> an impotent people
> Sick with inbreeding,
> Worrying the carcase of an old song.

In poems such as 'Reservoirs', writing about "the smell of decay/ from the putrefying of a dead nation", he attacked the failure of the Welsh to resist the encroachment of English influence in their own land, but he reserved his greatest diatribes for the English themselves. "England, what have you done to make the speech/ My fathers used a stranger at my lips?" he asked in 'The Old Language'.

R S Thomas had always been a patriot. One of the reasons why he moved from Manafon in Montgomeryshire, where he had been rector for twelve years, to Cardiganshire in 1954 and to Aberdaron in 1967 was to get closer to real Welsh Wales. However, it also brought him closer to English settlers who, as he saw it, were threatening the Welsh way of life. He became increasingly outspoken in his political views, attracting widespread condemnation for appearing to condone the burning of English holiday homes in Welsh-speaking areas. Paradoxically, he had his only son educated at an English public school and although he had learnt Welsh (and wrote his autobiography *Neb* – 'Nobody' – in that language) he never seriously attempted to write poetry in Welsh.

So, what is R S Thomas doing in a book about Welsh national heroes? Some would no doubt argue that the very ferocity of his patriotism justifies his inclusion. Many more would concede that through his poetry he has at least challenged the Welsh to consider who they are and where they are going. In the words of the *Western Mail*, never an uncritical admirer, on the occasion of his death: "At a time of lightning-fast change, which threatened to consign some of our most cherished cultural traditions to history, he was our conscience."

Moreover, he was a quite superb poet. He might well have received the Nobel Prize for Literature in 1996 had Seamus Heaney, another combative Celt, not won the accolade the year before. He did receive the Heinemann Prize for Poetry, the Queen's Gold Medal for Poetry, the Cholmondley Award and three Welsh Arts Council Awards. Not all his poems were harsh; some were compassionate, uplifting. All were memorable. Read them aloud. Above all, read 'A Marriage', a tender tribute to his late first wife.

DYLAN THOMAS
(1914–1953)

Dylan Thomas' middle name was Marlais after the bardic name of
William Thomas (Gwilym Marles), a nineteenth-century radical
Unitarian minister, an authentic Welsh hero and Dylan's great uncle.
Nevertheless, some may well wonder what qualifies Dylan Thomas of
all people to appear in a book of Welsh national heroes. He hardly cut a
heroic figure during his lifetime and his relationship with the land of his
birth was always rather complex. "Land of my fathers. My fathers can
keep it!" he once famously remarked, though in fairness there can be
few Welshmen who, at some time or other, have not displayed a degree
of exasperation with the parochialism sometimes shown by their
countrymen.

There is no doubt that Dylan's Welsh identity was important to
him. "One, I am a Welshman; two, I am a drunkard; three, I am a lover
of the human race, especially of women" was another of his well-known
sayings. Certainly there is hardly a Welshman better known throughout
the world and few modern poems have had a greater impact on the
English-speaking world than "Do not go gentle into that good night",
addressed to his dying father. This piece alone, with the line "rage, rage
against the dying of the light", which has powerfully captured for
generations of people the essence of the human condition, is sufficient
to elevate Dylan Thomas to the status of hero in the minds of many.
And who can fail to be moved by the Reverend Eli Jenkins' prayer in
Dylan's play for voices, *Under Milk Wood*, his best-known work, first
broadcast by the BBC shortly after his poignant death in a New York
hotel caused by chronic over-indulgence.

It is undeniable that Wales had a profound impact on Dylan's writing. *Fern Hill* was inspired by his Swansea childhood, and the 'Llareggub' of *Under Milk Wood* owed everything to two of his favourite places, New Quay and Laugharne. Indeed it is generally acknowledged that it was in the Boat House at Laugharne that he wrote much of his best work, looking out over the estuary from his writing shed, producing wonderfully evocative poems like 'Over Sir John's Hill', 'Poem on his Birthday', and, of course, 'Do not go gentle'. Then it was time to stroll over to Brown's Hotel for a few drinks, a gossip and a game of cards.

After his death he was brought back to Britain in the hold of the *SS United States* where his widow, Caitlin, watched while members of the crew played cards on his coffin. Dylan's burial in St Martin's churchyard, Laugharne, was a famously chaotic occasion. Never a conventional mourner Caitlin was sorely tempted to leap into Dylan's open grave because it would have looked "pretty sensational". She did indeed join her husband much later. After her death in Sicily she was buried with Dylan in August 1994, surrounded by hundreds of onlookers, including many curious holidaymakers dressed in their best beachwear. Their grave is in the middle of the annexe to the churchyard, prominently marked by a white wooden cross.

LAURA ASHLEY
(1925–1985)

With her husband, Laura Ashley (*née* Mountney) created a
multinational business empire which literally spread the name of Wales
throughout the world.

Laura was born in Dowlais Top (31 Station Terrace now carries a
commemorative plaque) and although brought up in London she spent
her childhood holidays with 'Grandma Wales' back in Merthyr Tydfil
where she acquired a deep and lifelong affection for the essentials of the
Welsh way of life. On Sundays she would attend Hebron Baptist
chapel, loving the atmosphere even if she could not understand a word
of the service. She was briefly evacuated back to Merthyr when war
broke out.

From small beginnings in London when she and her husband
Bernard (whom she had married in 1949) set up a textile-printing
business in 1953, they moved to Mid Wales in 1961 and proceeded to
create a major international enterprise, revitalising the local economy.
Both deserved to share the credit for the company's success and Laura
once refused the OBE because she believed that Bernard should have
been honoured too. Nevertheless, the brilliantly successful 'Laura Ashley
look', pastoral and resolutely traditional, was very much a reflection of
Laura's own view of life, significantly shaped by her childhood
experiences in Wales. "Respectability matters a lot to me," she
once said.

From their factories on the site of Carno railway station and
elsewhere in Mid Wales Laura Ashley clothes and fabrics, carrying the
'Made in Wales' label, were distributed throughout the world. In the

company's annual report for 1986 Bernard Ashley declared that "on average there is now a 'Laura Ashley' shop opening somewhere in the world at least once a week". By 1990 the Laura Ashley company had nearly 500 shops worldwide.

Sadly, Laura never saw the venture at the height of its success for she had been killed in a fall at her daughter's Cotswolds home in 1985. Though a reluctant tax exile since 1978 and residing in the Bahamas at the time of her death, it was entirely natural that she should be buried in the churchyard of St John the Baptist, in Carno, the location of the main Laura Ashley factory, surrounded by hundreds of mourners, and to the sound of the Dowlais Male Choir of which she had been vice-president.

CARWYN JAMES
(1929–1983)

In the early 1970s Gwynfor Evans called Carwyn James "the best-known Welshman in the world". Though proud of his family roots in Rhydlewis Carwyn was born and bred in the Carmarthenshire mining community of Cefneithin, attending Gwendraeth Secondary School with distinction (head boy, rugby captain and captain of the Welsh Secondary Schools XV). He studied Welsh at University College of Wales, Aberystwyth, where he began a lifelong commitment to Plaid Cymru, even contesting Llanelli for the party in the 1970 General Election. He won a respectable 8,500 votes, or as he later put it, "the average gate at Llanelli's Stradey Park".

Between 1957 and 1969 he was housemaster at Llandovery College, probably the happiest period of his life, before becoming a lecturer at Trinity College, Carmarthen, for a further five years (his referees were those literary giants Gwenallt and T H Parry-Williams), a post which gave him the freedom he needed to pursue his main interest.

Carwyn had been a successful fly-half with Llanelli in the 1950s and had won two Welsh caps (unfortunately Cliff Morgan was around at the same time), but it was as a rugby coach, the greatest of his generation, that he made his name. It was under him that Llanelli achieved a historic victory (9-3) against the All Blacks on 31 October 1972, and went on to dominate the Welsh rugby scene for the next few years. However, his greatest achievement was as the coach of the British Lions during their victorious tour of New Zealand in 1971. His planning was meticulous and he had the great teacher's gift of bringing the very best out of his players, recognising their individual talents and

earning their total commitment and respect.

To his everlasting disappointment the greatest prize of all eluded him. Characteristically the Welsh Rugby Union lacked the vision to make this rather complex character (who had already refused the offer of an MBE from the English Establishment) the coach of the Welsh XV and, apart from a couple of years coaching in Italy his last years were mainly spent as a highly regarded journalist and television pundit. Tormented by eczema Carwyn, a rather solitary man, found increasing solace in drink and cigarettes (untipped Senior Service, doubtless a legacy of his national service in the Navy) and died, alone, of a heart attack, in an Amsterdam hotel in January 1983, at the age of 53, leaving Welsh, and world rugby, stunned.

The man who, in Barry John's view, had the finest rugby brain he had ever known, was cremated at Morriston ten days later, his ashes scattered to the winds.

JOHN CHARLES
(born 1931)

John Charles is without doubt Wales' greatest ever footballer. Indeed many regard him as the finest British footballer of his generation, equally at home at the heart of the defence or leading the attack.

Born in Swansea and starting his career as a ground staff apprentice with Swansea Town he joined Leeds United in 1947, making his League debut two years later at the age of nineteen. Initially an imposing centre half, John's impressive pace led to his club manager, Major Frank Buckley, converting him into a centre forward with spectacular results. In 1952/3, his first year in that position, he scored 30 goals. In the following season he scored 42 goals in 39 games, a club record, and between 1949 and 1956 he played 279 games for Leeds, scoring 150 goals.

In 1956 John Charles became the first, and still the most successful, soccer export to Italy joining Juventus of Turin for what was then the largest transfer fee in British football history, £65,000. In his first full year, 1957/8, he scored 29 goals, taking Juventus to the Serie A championship and earning for himself the accolade of Italian Footballer of the Year. In 1960 and 1961 Juventus were League champions again and altogether, in 155 games during his career with Juventus, he scored 93 goals. It is hardly surprising that he was, and still is, revered in Italy as *'Il Buono Gigante'*, the 'Gentle Giant'. In 1961 the secretary of the Italian Football League, clearly forgetting the contributions of the Romans and Giacomo Bracchi to the social history of Wales, went so far as to say "Wales should give John Charles a medal. He has put it on the map. Nobody in Italy knew where it was before." He played for

Wales with great distinction 38 times, scoring 15 goals, including one against Hungary during the 1958 World Cup finals in Sweden.

From 1962 the rest of his playing career was something of an anti-climax. His best days were behind him. A brief return to Leeds (when the entrance charges were, for a few matches, tripled in an unpopular attempt to recoup some of the £53,000 the club had paid for him) was followed by spells with Roma, Cardiff City, Hereford Town and finally Merthyr Tydfil where he ended his playing career in 1972.

Since then Wales' finest football ambassador, who was never sent off or even cautioned during his football career, has confronted business failure and ill-health with characteristic dignity. "Only grandfathers remember me now," he once said, ruefully, but he was wrong. In 1999 the University of Wales gave him an Honorary MA and in the Queen's Birthday Honours List of 2001 he was belatedly awarded the CBE for services to football. "It's about time," said Cliff Jones, one of John's contemporaries, and there can be few who would disagree with his opinion.

HOWARD WINSTONE
(1939–2000)

In 1958 Cardiff hosted the 6th Empire and Commonwealth Games
and Wales finished seventh in the medal table with eleven medals, seven
bronze, three silver and one gold. Howard Winstone, from Merthyr
Tydfil, winner of the bantamweight gold medal became a Welsh
sporting legend overnight and retained the admiration of the Welsh
people for the rest of his life. He has been hailed as a hero by no less an
authority than Dafydd Iwan in a contribution to a book about Welsh
sporting giants, *Cewri Campau Cymru*.

Having turned professional in the following year Howard Winstone was to fight sixty-seven bouts between 1959 and 1968 under the skilful management of another great son of Merthyr Tydfil, Eddie Thomas, winning sixty-one of them, including the British featherweight championship in 1961 (against Terry Spinks) and the European crown in 1963. He was never known as a fearsome hitter. When he was seventeen he had lost three fingers of his right hand in an accident at a Merthyr toy factory and this undoubtedly impaired his punching power. Nevertheless, half of his sixty-one victims were stopped inside the distance, worn down by the constant jabs and counter-punches of a supreme boxing stylist.

In his quest for the World championship Howard was gallantly defeated three times by the Mexican Vincente Saldivar and many pundits (even Saldivar himself) considered that he had won the second epic contest at Ninian Park, Cardiff, in the summer of 1967. However, he was to beat Japan's Mitsuori Seki for the vacant title at the Albert Hall in January 1968, only to lose it to Jose Legra six months later, after which he retired from the ring.

Howard Winstone was awarded the MBE in 1968 and despite a series of failed business ventures he retained the affection of the Welsh sporting public and particularly of the people of Merthyr Tydfil, becoming a Freeman of the borough. Indeed Merthyr was brought to a standstill on the day of his funeral, when thousands gathered to pay their respects to one of the town's greatest ever ambassadors. A year later the world of boxing and the people of Merthyr again turned out in force to witness the unveiling, in St Tydfil's shopping centre, of a statue of Howard Winstone wearing two Lonsdale belts, sculpted by David Petersen, the son of another Welsh boxing legend, the great Jack Petersen.

**– Wales within your reach:
an attractive series
at attractive prices!**

Titles already published:

1. Welsh Talk
Heini Gruffudd
086243 447 5
£2.95

2. Welsh Dishes
Rhian Williams
086243 492 0
£2.95

3. Welsh Songs
Lefi Gruffudd (ed.)
086243 525 0
£3.95

4. Welsh Mountain Walks
Dafydd Andrews
086243 547 1
£3.95

5. Welsh Organic Recipes
Dave and Barbara Frost
086243 574 9
£3.95

6. Welsh Railways
Jim Green
086243 551 X
£3.95

7. Welsh Place Names
Brian Davies
086243 514 5
£3.95

8. Welsh Castles
Geraint Roberts
086243 550 1
£3.95

9. Welsh Rugby Heroes
Androw Bennett
086243 552 8
£3.95

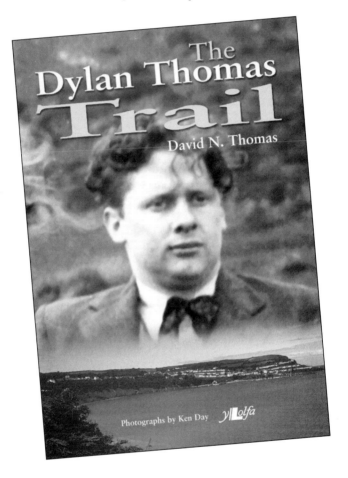

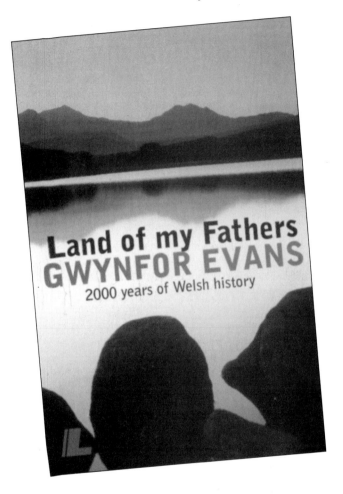

A masterful history of the Welsh nation by the most distinguished
Welsh politician of the twentieth century; 500 pages.

£12.95
ISBN: 0 86243 265 0

The *It's Wales* series
is just one of a wide range
Welsh interest publications
from Y Lolfa.
For a full list of books currently in print,
send now for your free copy
of our new, full-colour Catalogue
– or simply surf into our website
at **www.ylolfa.com.**

Talybont Ceredigion Cymru/*Wales* SY24 5AP
ffôn 0044 (0)1970 832 304 *ffacs* 832 782 *isdn* 832 813
e-bost ylolfa@ylolfa.com *y we* www.ylolfa.com